THE SACRED FOREST

THE SACRED

— *Pierre-Dominique Gaisseau*

TRANSLATED FROM THE FRENCH BY STEPHEN BECKER

FOREST

MAGIC AND SECRET RITES IN FRENCH GUINEA

NEW YORK: ALFRED A. KNOPF: 1954

THIS IS A BORZOI BOOK, PUBLISHED BY ALFRED A. KNOPF, INC.

L. C. catalog card number: 54–7204

FIRST AMERICAN EDITION

Originally published in France as FORÊT SACRÉE, *copyright 1953 by Editions Albin Michel.*

TO

VOINÉ KOIWOGUI / ZÉZÉ SOHOWOGUI / WEGO BEAWOGUI

Toma witch-doctors who made this book possible

EXCERPT *from a letter to Pierre-Dominique Gaisseau by the Governor of French Guinea*

NUMBER 38 APA   28 May 1953

Dear Sir:

I have the honor to inform you that as a result of the unrest among the Toma of the Gueriguerika caused by your filming and recording the rites of their fetish cult, the sight of which is forbidden to women and to non-initiates, I have found it necessary to cancel the authorization granted you in order number 839 of 25 February last.

(SIGNED) P. I.

Governor

FOREWORD

The structure of this book may seem ingenuous. I am neither a professional writer nor a professional ethnologist, and in relating the experiences of four Frenchmen who lived for a few months the life of an African tribe I have simply followed the chronological order of events.

During the early part of our stay we traveled through the territory of the Toma tribe, noting on the wing words and actions the significance of which escaped us more often than not. Rather than continue about our work as simple spectators, we undertook to integrate ourselves into the Toma community and to conform to its way of life. Only after our initiation were we capable of trying to fathom Toma ethics and the sense of Toma traditions.

In the latter part of this book, then, is an attempted unification, a synthesis of observations from notes, recordings, photographs, and moving pictures brought back; it will, I hope, complete or confirm certain theories, and perhaps even add fresh material to our present knowledge of Africa.

Three Toma witch-doctors consented to let us see, and film, their secret ceremonies, and to let us undergo ourselves the rites of initiation; but all the others, angered by this sacrilege, invoked ancestral laws and roused the Toma people against us. Following upon this collective demonstration of hostility, the French government of Guinea, in order to avoid further local manifestations, ordered us to suspend our work, in a letter that confirms the authenticity of the reports, written and filmed,* that we brought out.

Although grave threats still hang over our witch-doctor friends, guilty of having revealed to us the secrets of their tribe, we have recently been notified that they are still alive and will not suffer too much from the consequences of our effort.

* The reader's attention is called to an album of photographs which follows page 152.

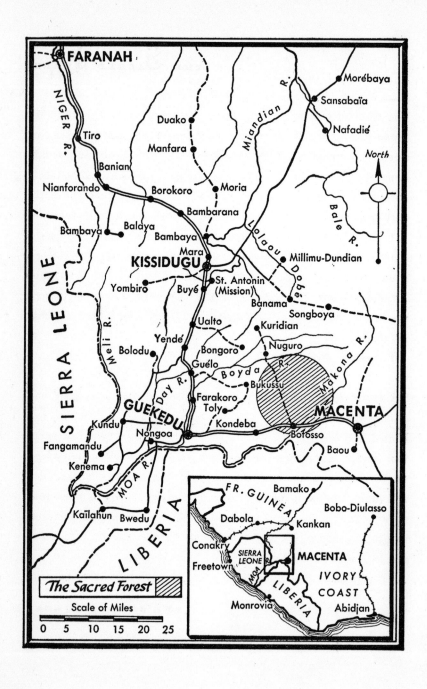

FARANAH

Morébaya
Sansabaïa
Nafadié

Duako
Manfara

NIGER R.
Tiro
Banian
Nianforando
Borokoro
Moria
Bambarana
Balaya
Bambaya
Bambaya
Mara
KISSIDUGU
St. Antonin
(Mission)
Yombiro
Buyé
Banama
Millimu-Dundian
Songboya
Ualto
Kuridian
Yendé
Bongoro
Nuguro
Bolodu
Guélo
Boyda R.
Bukussu
MACENTA
Farakoro
Toly
GUEKEDU
Kondeba
Kundu
Nongoa
Botósso
Fangamandu
Baou
Kenema

SIERRA LEONE

Meli R.

Day R.

MOAR R.

Makona R.

Miandian R.

Bale R.

Lolaou Dobé

North

Kaïlahun
Bwedu

LIBERIA

The Sacred Forest
Scale of Miles
0   5   10   15   20   25

FR. GUINEA
Bamako
Bobo-Diulasso
Dabola
Kankan
Conakry
SIERRA
LEONE
MACENTA
Freetown
MOA R.
IVORY
COAST
LIBERIA
Monrovia
Abidjan

ONE

The Chevrolet pick-up truck ground along through the night between two high walls of vegetation. The winding, bumpy road rose steadily. A moonless sky was studded with frozen stars; in this latitude they gleamed with a steady brilliance. Now and then the black, abrupt peaks of the Futa-Jallon range came into view above the dark mass of forest; we were climbing slowly through the foothills.

From time to time the silhouette of a small animal, crossing the road in one leap, or the curve of a huge branch, suddenly detached from the dense brush, appeared in the beam of the headlights. Around us, over the constant stridulation of innumerable insects, rose the forest's great night-music; even the roar of the motor could not drown it out.

For us the adventure had at last begun.

Six days before, on February 16, 1953, we had left Paris by air, and after a quick flight over Morocco and the Saharan coast we had landed in Conakry, the capital of French Guinea. We had spent four days in that ultramodern boom-town of many-colored buildings, where enormous bauxite refineries and iron-smelters worked day and night, like immense mechanized ant-hills. It took us those four days to wangle the necessary authorization to take motion pictures, and to clear ourselves with the customs people. On the fifth morning, by chance, we had run across the truck-driver.

"If you can squeeze in there with all your baggage," he said, pointing to the narrow platform, "I'll take you to Kissidugu. You can pick up another truck there for Macenta. It's on the coffee run."

Kissidugu was about five hundred miles east of Conakry, on the outskirts of the tropical forest; and the forest was our destination. Happy to take advantage of the opportunity, we managed to load our fragile technical equipment, after several attempts, and we were off early in the afternoon.

———

Surrounded by the crates, Virel and I took shelter in a kind of cave, protecting ourselves from the night wind that whipped across our faces in brutal contrast to the insufferable heat of the day. Sitting well back against the cab, and wrapped in blankets, we swapped first impressions of the expedition.

"I'd never have believed it could be this cold in Africa," Virel said.

The cold was only relative, the difference between day heat and night heat; I reminded Virel of a Christmas night near the source of the Orinoco, when, shivering under our blankets, teeth chattering, we had finally brought out the thermometer. It had read seventy-five degrees.

"It's probably sixty-five or seventy right now," Virel said. "But nobody could sleep on all these banknotes anyway."

We were, in fact, stretched out on jute sacks containing several million francs in bills of small denominations. The driver was taking them to Kissidugu to buy up the natives' coffee crop for the year. During the day he had gone to the bank to pick up the new, crackling bills, divided into thick bundles as hard as bricks. The inhabitants of the bush scorned wrinkled bills and sometimes refused to accept them.

Through the rear window of the cab I could see Jean Fichter dozing. Between his knees was a loaded rifle the driver had given him, in the very slim hope of dropping a hind, a peccary, or even a panther, in the beam of the headlights. Occasionally Jean's head nodded over onto Tony Saulnier's shoulder; Tony too was half-asleep. Good, that they were taking advantage of the cab's relative comfort; in a few hours they would spell us on the rigid mattress of banknotes.

Jean Fichter, my earliest companion in exploring (and my brother-in-law), combined the functions of head cameraman, sound-technician, and general mechanic. Together we had made the first crossing of the Serra Parima,* and shot the documentary of the Orinoco-Amazon expedition.

We had both had previous experience of Guinea; the year before, during a preliminary film survey, we had traveled the whole colony. With no private car, we had made use of local transport: small riverboats, trucks of the native carrier lines, single-track upcountry trains from Conakry to Kankan; and thanks to this rough-and-tumble transportation (packed into jabbering, motley crowds with bicycles, poultry, and assorted bundles) and to our stays in native villages in the bush, we had gradually learned something about the various regions of the whole vast territory and about the customs of its inhabitants.

In this colony, where transition was in full swing, where the in-

* A range along the border between southern Venezuela and northwestern Brazil, in which the Orinoco rises. (Translator's note.)

fluence of technological progress was felt more and more, a strange evolution was being sketched; and among its varied manifestations was the anarchic assimilation of the white man's language. The picturesque alterations it underwent, particularly outside the large cities, were at first astonishing.

A year before, on the train to Kankan, we had been discussing the evolution of the natives, in some detail, with an African official. In a Homburg, a black jacket with piping, and morning trousers, he further displayed (despite the crushing heat) a stiff collar and a gray bow-tie. He rose to greet a passing friend in the corridor, and rejoined us after a few moments.

"Excuse me, my very dear friends," he said courteously. "I was exchanging a few words with a most fortuitously encountered chum."

And as he took leave of us later, bowing very gracefully: "I thank you for the pleasure that your conversation has dispensed to me."

We had no trouble keeping straight faces. Even before, a young boy had introduced himself to us as "an orphan of both sexes"; and at the home of one of our friends we had read this letter from an employee of his:

> Dear Boss, a raise would be torridly indispensable to me, I have neither brother on my right side nor sister on my left side to help me, and on the contrary a poor multiparous mother of three young children under my responsibility. I am writing to you because I think above all else of my satisfaction.

THE SACRED FOREST

Throughout our trip we would continue to pick up samples of this renovated language.

Our route had taken us successively to the country of the Nalu, its islands of mud planted with mangroves, along the coast to the south; to the north, among the Bassari, a naked tribe living along the Senegal border; and finally across the Futa-Jallon range into the savanna inhabited by the Peuhls and the Islamic Malinkés, and beyond to Toma country, in southeast Guinea, along the Liberian frontier. There, with the mountains, begins the dense forest, where lianas spread an impenetrable network under a thick canopy of giant trees, and where rounded crests rise like huge black turtles.

There is only one true way to know the Toma country: cross it on foot, with bearers. The innumerable rivers that slice through it, narrow and chopped up by rapids, make navigation impossible and access difficult.

Farmers and hunters, the Toma cultivate mountain rice (their staple) and coffee. They harvest the fruit of the palm-oil tree, which grows wild in the forest; and they raise a few head of domesticated stock.

All the way across Guinea we had heard fantastic tales of Toma magic, and of their great masks. But we were fascinated particularly by the sacred wood, their temple of sorcerery, a sanctuary outside each village where secret rites, barbaric ceremonies of initiation, and at times even human sacrifices still took place.

In March 1951 Jean Fichter and I had arrived in Macenta, the only European town in the region. The police commissioner filled in our skeleton of information as well as he could, allowed us to consult the official archives, and even told us of a few strange events he had witnessed. One of those events struck us with special force; the commissioner was unable to explain it. A few months before, during a trip through the bush, a geologist had suddenly collapsed and died at the commissioner's side; this, after having ignored the witch-doctors' warnings and climbed a boulder sacred to the Toma.

The commissioner showed us documents on ritual crimes, now become rare, and, among his array of now ancient evidence, a large black mask about a yard high. He promised to turn it over to us when we left, for delivery to the Musée de l'Homme in Paris.

"If you want to film masks like this," he had added, "you'll have to wait for one of the big ceremonies. Normally, you don't see these otherwise. There ought to be one in a little while now, in a village on the road to Guekedu. Ask the district commissioner. He'll tell you about it."

This latter had received us very cordially, and had given us a letter of introduction to Kowo Guilawogui, who had just been named district chief in Kolibiramatoma. Thanks to that introduction, we had been able to film all the high ceremonies that marked the inauguration of the new chief. Kowo Guilawogui's dress had disconcerted us when he welcomed us to Niogbozu, his village. Warned in advance of our arrival, he was waiting for us in an immaculate white suit and a pith helmet. Tall and thin, he was about our age.

He did us the honors of his hut, and then led us to the one reserved for us. On the immense bed he had had installed were Oriental rugs, serving as blankets. Against the wall, cases of vintage champagne and demijohns of Beaujolais, ordered from Macenta in our honor, were lined up.

After presenting us to two or three of his wives, young and gracious in lively cotton prints, with necklaces and pendants in gold filigree, he led us before his mother. She was an aged woman, tall, erect, white-haired, with fine features and an imposing air. Though in Toma dress (a loincloth and nothing else), she lost nothing of her dignity.

Kowo had supervised the installation of a table, with a tablecloth, and we ate in the European manner. The cook, whom, like the wine, he had ordered from Macenta, prepared sophisticated specialties: roast chicken with pimento, and heart- or fish-shaped fritters.

Kowo had spent several years in Macenta and spoke almost perfect French. An attentive host, he sat with us through all our meals, but never shared them. He was satisfied to drink with us occasionally. Our amazement verged on disappointment. We had thought we were penetrating to the heart of the bush, and here we were in clover. There was only one shadow in the picture, a very light shadow: the tepidness of the champagne. It was practically at room temperature.

While the ceremonies lasted, he did all he could to help us in our work, and to let us film the large masks we had heard so much about. He admired our tape recorder exceedingly, and the natives of Niogbozu shared his enthusiasm for it. The day of our arrival we had recorded a speech by Kowo; the playback was a revelation to everyone. As the first words roared out of the speaker, he recognized his own voice, snapped to attention, and removed his helmet.

The next morning he agreed to take us to the sacred wood. Not far from the village, where the bush began, he stopped before a gateway of tangled fern roots, into which a narrow opening was cut.

"The entrance to the sacred wood," he announced.

No barrier extended to either side of this symbolic doorway. A small awning of palm fronds was tilted against the fern roots; beneath it, against a background of painted designs, stood small clay statues: effigies of the forest spirits.

I knew that entrance to this domain was forbidden to women and non-initiates, but I asked Kowo for permission to go on. After a brief conference with the dignitaries who had come with us, he gave this ambiguous reply:

"No. It's forbidden. But if you want to, you can."

Which meant, decoded: our laws forbid it, but white men can do anything. And which implied: you may cross the forbidden sill, but witch-doctors, warned by methods known only to themselves, will cause to vanish anything in the wood that might interest you.

I understood then that the domain was not in itself consecrated ground; that the paraphernalia of ritual worship, hidden there, hallowed it. If we had disregarded the interdict, we would simply have entered an abandoned church.

"Then we won't go in now," I said. "Later on, when you give us permission."

This evasive attitude on the part of a Toma who called himself our friend only increased our desire to learn the secrets of the wood. We badgered him with questions, and even offered to undergo the initiation rites if it would better our possibilities. Finally, after a few days, he made a concession. "All the elders and the people of the village trust you," he said, "but it's still too soon. You'll have to wait for the ceremonies at the initiates' return. Come back in a year. You'll be tattooed, and you'll live in the forest for a month, and you'll learn our secrets."

Then he told us that the Toma had noticed the whirring of the camera when we took pictures. So there was no chance of filming them without their knowledge.

On the way back to the coast, passing through Macenta, we and the police commissioner hunted vainly for the large black mask. It had disappeared, doubtless recovered by the Toma.

In Paris again, we kept in touch with the Toma country. Prosper Zumanigui, an African male nurse in Macenta who had been our interpreter, wrote often to give us news of Kowo and to keep us informed of preparations for the initiates' return. We sent him photographs and promised to bring back the film we had shot and run it off in Niogbozui; and we readied our next expedition, agreed upon even before we had left Guinea.

Two friends had joined us, meanwhile. Tony Saulnier was a reporter-photographer for *Match*, a specialist in African and Oceanian primitive art—calm, precise, painstaking in his work. He would help Jean Fichter and, if necessary, replace him.

André Virel, completely preoccupied by symbolism and primitive religions, wanted to check his theories against reality.

We had had to find a producer willing to trust us with the hazardous project—so hazardous that we had spoken of it only to our most intimate friends. We wanted not only to observe the secret rites of the Toma and to participate in them, but also to film them. We knew very well that any such project would be hard to realize, in spite of Kowo's promises. We were not impelled by simple curiosity, nor by the enthusiasm of the complete cameraman, but by the desire to enter a world different from our own and to understand it.

———

We prepared our equipment with special care and tried to foresee all eventualities, all possible breakdowns. We took two 35-mm. electric cameras, a generator, sixteen thousand feet of virgin black-and-white film, a projector, two tape recorders and the necessary tape, three Rolleiflexes, one Leica, one flash attachment, bulbs, and magnesium flares for night shooting. Trusting in Toma hospitality, we carried no arms and no food supplies. Our personal effects and camping equipment were reduced to the minimum.

In one of the crates was the film we had shot the year before; we were counting on it to convince Kowo that he ought to keep the promises he had made.

We were all in fine physical shape, and determined to succeed. On an expedition of this kind it would be hard to keep to schedule, but we had set a limit of two months to our stay, and hoped to be able to pull out before the rainy season began.

———

The road went on rising, in hairpin turns. The cold bit sharply. I twisted up off my invaluable mattress and glanced into the cab.

The driver turned.

"Haven't you had enough for a while?" I asked him. "We could take a break."

"Me? I drove all last night, too. I never sleep at the wheel."

The valley yawned before us. Beyond, high rocky cliffs stood out against a dark sky.

Suddenly, swinging into a curve, the truck jolted and jerked, bucking violently, out of control. With a last sharp shock, it rammed into the high shoulder.

I jumped to the cab window. The driver stared at me, bewildered. He had fallen asleep, with his head on the wheel. Now we were all awake, but we took advantage of the forced landing and caught a nap.

Wearing two sweaters, buried in my sleeping-bag, rolled in a blanket, I was shivering. Close around us the forest grated, quivered, croaked, rippled, whispered. I opened my eyes. Everywhere in the black curtain of trees pairs of luminous points, thousands of them, caught fire, and blinked, and died, and caught fire again.

Virel was awake next to me. By the distance between their eyes we tried to identify the rodents and insects watching us so motionlessly from the forest. Gradually we dozed off again.

Two hours later, dawn woke us. A pale, clear dawn; the sun rose very quickly.

Under a dazzling blue sky, of the kind I had seen only at high altitudes, we headed for the plateau of the Futa-Jallon. Savanna stretched to the horizon, continually scorched, continually freshening to a new green; the skeletons of burnt-out trees rose from it.

CHAPTER ONE

The driver kept us below forty miles an hour; otherwise the truck would have been a heap of spare parts in no time. As it was, we were shaken like cocktails on the narrow platform for hours on end.

Although lessened, the jolting pounded our equipment sorely; as soon as we arrived we would have to check it all, tightening bolts and resoldering connections.

We crossed the Niger over a bridge laid on canoes. Here, near its source, the river was hardly wider than the Loire. The water was clear and shallow. We were still in the dry season.

That night we saw the first clumps of trees around Kissidugu, where the forest began. In two days, if brush fires didn't hold us up, or fallen bridges, or mechanical breakdowns, we would see Kowo again.

TWO

I had never been so full of emotion while running off a film. The swollen, strident vibration of insects, which had risen unceasingly from the brush since dawn, seemed to have been silenced. I could only hear the buzzing of the projector. The credits were being flashed on the screen; what would these men of the forest think of films shot last year here in their own village?

The whole cast was there that night, assembled in the small village square. Men, women, children, the aged: packed pell-mell into the square, they sat on the ground, their uneasy, attentive faces turned to the screen hung from a hut. Kowo alone, lordly, took his ease on a chair—a low chair, of carved wood. He was surrounded by village dignitaries. Innumerable bright-eyed children waited tensely, like children in the Luxembourg Gardens impatient for the puppet show.

The opening scenes ran off in an agonizing silence; then suddenly the first laughter, the first gleeful shouts, rang out. They had recognized themselves. At the sight of Kowo being carried triumphantly around the village in his palanquin, there was wild enthusiasm. I stepped away from the projector toward Kowo and leaned over his shoulder.

"You look pleased," I said. "Everything all right?"

"Fine, fine," he said impatiently, not taking his eyes off the screen.

He had just appeared in the foreground, supporting the horns of

THE SACRED FOREST

a huge ram whose throat had been cut. The dignitaries in the background were watching him with alert expressions; he must then have been feeling the power of the ram and the touch of death pass into himself.

I was a bit baffled by the spectator reaction. In Paris, ritual sacrifices of cocks, rams, and bulls, on the tomb of old Badé, Kowo's father, had provoked horrified shudders and occasionally loud protests; here they aroused shouts of enthusiasm. There was no cruelty in this glee, though. The Toma are skilled in the reading of omens, in watching the fall of kola nuts thrown before sacrificial victims. And these scenes proved that the sacrifices had succeeded, had "been accepted," and that Badé's soul was satisfied.

The Wenilegagui, the bird-men, appeared on the screen: two balls of stiff feathers, supported by long, muscular legs, and topped by white, tragic faces, painted in white lime, under high tail-feathers. Hopping in place to a frenzied rhythm, side by side or face to face, heads thrown back, they performed a series of ritual movements with incredible agility; their caller was a drummer with a tiny wooden tom-tom. This drumbeat code was one of the secret languages of the forest.

I left Kowo deep in his mute contemplation, and took up a position near the screen. From there I watched the flickering light of the projector play on their mobile faces.

Suddenly the children shrieked, terrified, clinging to those next them or to the women squatting behind them, who had also shrunk back. They had just seen the huge black Bakorogui masks, fringed with goat-hair, some of them with human hair; the masks were dancing ponderously through the village. These were the guardians of the sacred wood, nemesis to women and non-initiates.

Finally the Laniboi appeared in his flexible black mask haloed with white fur, under a witch-doctor's dappled hat. Perched on ten-foot stilts hidden by his long, striped minstrel-show pants, he crossed the village square in three strides, his arms flung wide; he glided along at roof-top height, pretended to fall, caught himself up, and spun like a top on one leg. The whole audience was ecstatic at the antics of this winged giant.

With no transition, the gateway to the sacred wood succeeded him on the screen. A long murmur rose from the crowd. I understood then that for the Toma this was not simply a change of scene in the film, but a miracle. The Laniboi and the masks that had preceded it were actually, for them, incarnations ("nephews," they called them), visible to everyone, of the Afwi, the Great Spirit that inhabits the sacred wood.

Discreetly I slipped back into the last row of spectators. I had expected to be bombarded with questions; they were not even aware that I was near them.

On the screen strange beings were gliding slowly among the huts and the tombs: the Guelemlai, forest messengers. Skulls shaven, bodies whitened with lime, their shoulders supported a wide basket-work horse-collar, from which long fringes of gilded raffia hung. Armed with long white poles, holding their torsos stiff, they crossed the silent village in long skaters' strides. Their dance had to be entirely unaccompanied by music. Then they disappeared into the forest shadows. Around me several women drew back their headscarves; they had covered their faces at the sight of these phantoms.

The film had ended. The audience was talking it over animatedly. I went to find Kowo. He hugged me mightily. Tears ran down his face. "Thank you, thank you," he said. "I want to see it again."

A few dignitaries approached. They made wide gestures. Kowo translated their astonishment for me. It was the huge enlargement of the kola nut that had stunned them.

"How do you do it," he asked, his arms spread, "make them so big?"

We had to run the film four times. The Toma's enthusiasm was boundless. We could have gone on until dawn.

Now the village square was deserted; after showing their pleasure once more, the natives had gone back to their huts. We had not seen Kowo again; would he still be willing to keep his promises?

Not knowing just why, I doubted it; listening to the eternal murmur of the bush, I mulled over the question for a long while, unable to sleep.

The next morning Kowo avoided us. He had the village chief bring us the ritual gifts: a live chicken, rice, and a gourd full of palm wine. But he did not appear himself. In the large guest hut, reserved for us this year as it had been the year before, we fretted, stretched out on hammocks we had brought back from the Amazon country.

In Africa hurrying was out of the question, and we had no wish to compromise our chances of success by impatience; we could only let Kowo make the decision in his own good time. To while away the time Jean and I guided our two friends, new to the country, through Niogbozu. We felt a proprietary pride; what we wanted most was to have our friends appreciate the beauty and cleanliness of this typical Toma village.

At their doorsills the women, wearing striped loincloths, their breasts bare, were pounding rice with slow, regular motions. They raised the heavy pestles, six feet tall, and let them fall to the mortars. Resonant shocks of wood against wood echoed from one hut to another; the tom-tom rhythm swelled through the village.

Old men, draped in blue-and-white-striped tunics, lounged on chaise-longues of their own manufacture and chewed tobacco in the sun. A girl, lying prone, knees bent, feet in the air, her head against the thighs of a kneeling woman, lazily was having her hair done.

We ran across a few friends of the year before; we shook hands in the Toma manner, with light slaps of our fingers against their palms.

Squeezed one against another and crowned with thatch, the round white huts of Niogbozu stood like beehives in their enclave of red earth. The tall tropical forest, the soaring, spongy trunks of silk-cotton trees, hemmed them in closely.

In Toma country the dead are buried among the living; here and there among the huts lay the black slabs of tombs, bordered by standing stones. On the outskirts of the village a new hut was under construction. Three men whom Jean and I recognized finished braiding the branches that would serve as framework for the circular adobe wall. The conical skeleton of the roof was already in place, awaiting only its thatch covering. Near the door, against the wall, was a platform of tamped earth; covered by a simple straw mat, it would become a Toma bed.

Niogbozu, like all Toma agglomerations, was situated atop a hill; a circle of lianas, tied end to end and left on the ground, marked the village limits. The trails into the village were good thoroughfares, wide and well kept, mounting the steep slope.

Outside the circle of lianas, at the forest's edge, a small native forge had been set up, under a thatched roof supported by thin columns. A black rock was the anvil. The Toma do not know how to extract iron from the granular laterite of the soil; but they know how to work it. They obtain it from the Malinkés, their neighbors, in the form of *guinzé,* thin metal strips twisted spirally and flattened at either end; these strips are used both as money * and as raw material for the manufacture of arms and tools.

In the square the weavers looked as though they had not budged since the year before. Sap had begun to circulate again through the wooden posts planted at their doorsteps to support looms; the weavers bent over their cloth in the shadow of new leaves. During my first trip I had suggested that they widen the weft of their woven cotton, but the idea must have struck them as ridiculous; they had continued to weave bands of blue, yellow, and white cotton, hardly four inches wide, several of which sewn together made up flowing, striped tunics, their most common garment.

Sitting back against the wall of a hut, two elders were playing *fao,*

* A *guinzé* is worth about five francs, or one cent and a half.

nimbly moving seeds in an oval wooden plate crisscrossed by deep grooves. We stood watching them for a while, trying to work out the rules of this African backgammon, but failed completely.

The village resounded with the hammering of pestles: the women were still husking rice, their staple, for the noon meal. We had not yet run into Kowo. I made up my mind to go and see him.

He was not alone in his hut. Wearing a red turban he had recently adopted as a symbol of high position, he was surrounded by goat-bearded elders with white hair twisted into short braids; a bitter argument was under way. I guessed the subject of the conference immediately: all conversation ceased as I entered.

We exchanged the usual greetings. *"Iche, icheyo . . . imama, mamayo."*

But silence fell again, and the atmosphere remained hostile. True, these polite formulas corresponded exactly to our "Hello, how are you?" and might indicate indifference as easily as hypocrisy.

After a painful moment Kowo gestured; he wanted to speak to me outside. He seemed even less at ease than the others, and I followed him, a little anxious.

After assuring me once again of his many debts of gratitude to us, and insisting on his warm regard for us, he got down to facts: one month before we arrived, white men had desecrated the sacred wood, making off with a ritual mask. The witch-doctors' fury was now directed at all foreigners. They were more than ever determined to keep their secrets inviolate. They did not understand the whites' interest in the sacred wood, and refused us permission to enter.

Kowo was young. Although he was their chief, he could not defy the will of the elders. "The old men have the last word," he said in a hollow, solemn voice. "I can't do any more for you."

Our conversation had led us outside the village, to the gateway of the sacred wood. The year before, too, we had been stopped there; I refused to quit now.

I insisted: "I've brought you the films and photographs, as I promised. I've come all the way from Paris, with all that equipment, for this one purpose. You've got to do something."

Kowo hesitated and looked away. "I've done all I can."

I glanced up at the twisted black fern roots winding up over the gateway. Beyond them lay the forbidden world; only a few steps separated me from it. And in spite of myself I raised my voice:

"That can't be, Kowo. You've got to try again."

My anger surprised him; he had never seen me in that state. He stared at me for a long moment, perplexed, almost hurt.

"If you want," he said finally, "I'll call the elders together tonight. You can talk to them yourself."

On that he left me and joined the witch-doctors waiting for him at his hut.

Of course we had known when we planned the expedition that the Toma would set obstacles between us and their magical universe. But at least Kowo was sincere. I knew him well enough to be sure of his good faith. Still, where he had failed, with all his prestige and authority, could we succeed?

The others had been waiting anxiously for the results of my talk with Kowo.

"Well?" Jean said.

All I could do was tell them the bad news. "Anyway, all the elders here know us. With a little luck, we'll work it out."

That much was true: we might, by our presence, manage to wipe out the bad impression left by the desecration of the sacred wood. That evening we would hear the witch-doctors' final decision; and we all showed more optimism than we felt.

———

The sun set rapidly. In small groups, discreetly, the elders entered Kowo's hut.

A woman crossed the village square, wearing only her *m'bila*, the G-string that all Toma women wear beneath their loincloths. She wore no head-scarf, and her wild, frizzy hair was in stiff disorder. Wide spatters of dried mud lay like scales on her cheeks, her breasts, her belly, her thighs. Her face devoid of expression, she walked like an automaton, eyes glazed. She held a green branch in each hand. A female mourner followed her; at the door of each hut, she announced the death of an old woman in a near-by village.

Full night fell, and still we waited, sitting in a silent circle at our own doorsill. In the elders' hut the discussion was becoming heated. Occasionally we heard sharp outbursts and recognized Kowo's gloomy voice. We understood no Toma, but we knew that he was defending us, battering at the elders' ignorance and fanaticism.

Abruptly, silence. The door opened. Kowo's tall, thin figure appeared in the doorway. Slowly he crossed the square. His pace alone gave us our answer. All hope was gone. As he approached, I raised my lantern. His dark, gleaming face betrayed a great lassitude. There were tears in his eyes.

"Come," he said simply. "The elders will speak to you."

In the semidarkness of the hut the small yellow flame of the lantern threw their faces into relief. They all seemed dejected, but resolute. An old man stepped toward me. Kowo translated as the old man spoke, and hardly even had to grope for words.

"We know you," the elder said; "you are not whites like the other whites. We would like to help you. But the secrets of the Toma are for the Toma alone . . . a white man is a white man, a black man is a black man . . . we can do nothing for you."

There was nothing to say. I knew that their decision was irrevocable. I left. Kowo followed me. We walked along side by side in the deserted, moonlit village, saying nothing. A muted song rose from a distant hut: a women's choir, the rattle of gourds marking the rhythm. Kowo answered my unspoken question:

"The dead woman's relatives, wailing."

Slowly we returned to the large hut. Through the open doorway I saw my three friends, sitting in hammocks, their legs hanging; no one spoke.

Kowo drew back. He did not want to come in, to continue a fruitless argument. He murmured a rapid "Good night," and was gone.

Jean looked up at me. "A year of work for that," he said, shrugging. He had spoken for all of us.

At dawn we pulled out of Niogbozu. Two Guelemlai, like angels of death, crossed the square slowly as we left.

———

When we reached Macenta, early in the afternoon, we got hold of the district commissioner. He was hardly surprised to hear about our troubles with Kowo and the elders. He even advised us strongly to give up our plans, and to go shoot our film in some other region. While we were making up our minds, he would quarter us in an empty hut at the top of the hill that dominated Macenta.

Morale was low. We were wondering dismally around the sunny market place when I recognized a familiar figure. It was Prosper Zumanigui, our interpreter of the year before. We had never stopped thinking of him as a friend, and held a happy reunion on the spot.

Prosper was now chief male nurse at the hospital, in the trypanosome ward, where they treated the ever rarer cases of sleeping sickness. He promised to drop by at our hut during the evening.

High on the hill, our spacious hut was divided into two rooms, each furnished with a huge square bed; but mattress stuffing was nonexistent. We were tired and depressed, and none of us was cheerful enough to string up his hammock.

At dusk Prosper showed up. Sitting out in front of the hut, we told him the whole story. The tiny lights of Macenta winked in the valley at our feet.

Prosper thought it over carefully before commenting. "Anyway," he said, "you couldn't shoot the initiates' return. The witch-doctors have postponed it again. But in Soguru, north of the road to Guekedu, it's almost time for the mass tattooing of the children, before they send them into the sacred wood."

With that unexpected possibility, morale rose perceptibly.

"Yes," Prosper said, "but to see it you'd have to be tattooed yourselves."

Sleepless, I twisted on the too hard mattress for over an hour trying to find a tolerable position. Even then I had to wiggle quietly, so as not to awaken Jean, who was sharing the bed with me.

Wide-eyed in the darkness, I considered Prosper's last statement: "You'd have to be tattooed yourselves." The year before, Kowo had talked about putting us through that test. And hardly two days ago he had evaded all my questions on the subject. Was the initiation indispensable? How accessible was it to a white man? No matter; we would not lose this latest opportunity; we would be there for the ceremony.

Suddenly I sat up, listening. A strange music became audible over the familiar mutterings of the forest at night. Three high flute-notes and the crystal tinkling of a tiny bell drifted around the hut. Now close, now distant, the sounds seemed to come from different points at each instant. Holding my breath, I hesitated to wake Jean. Finally I grabbed his shoulder and shook him, but it was Virel's voice that answered, from the other side of the partition:

"You hear that?"

We got up and murmured together in the darkness. Tony refused to come fully awake. These unnerving manifestations had no effect on him.

"Leave me 'lone," he said in a muddy voice. "Lemme sleep."

Jean felt the same way, but the strange music, persisting, led him to suggest a strenuous procedure: man-hunt, if man there was; he would not, of course, take part himself.

We waited patiently in the gloom. When we thought the sounds were at their greatest volume, we leaped suddenly out of the hut, with the flashlight beamed in their presumed direction. The light revealed only stunted shrubbery among the grasses. The music had ceased.

We were hardly back in the hut when the haunting theme rose again, even louder.

Tony was severe in criticizing our tactics. "You should have crept out, very quietly and with no light."

"Why don't you give it a try yourself?"

"I happen to be asleep," he answered firmly.

We decided to follow his example and lay down again. The tiny flute and the bell continued their tantalizing round. Finally we dozed off; the music had not quit for a moment.

We had just arrived in Macenta, and Niogbozu was over thirty miles away. But all the Toma sorcerers knew our plans already. Tonight they had told us as much, for the first time.

———

We took our meals at the Caravansérail. In a town populated by Europeans, this was the name given to the hotel, or to what served a hotel's purpose. In Macenta it was a large rectangular hut with a thatched roof. An immense bar, fashioned of local wood and decorated by local sculptors with busts of Negroid American Indians, filled one end of the lounge.

After a few days we knew all the habitués: European or African

CHAPTER TWO

merchants and officials of the village. Tonight a newcomer caused a stir by the violence of his speeches. With the sincerity of an accomplished politician, he proclaimed his love of democracy, European civilization in general, and France in particular. Thin and elegant, he sported a soft shirt and a shining soft nylon hat. Gesturing freely, he approached our table.

In a state of advanced euphoria, he rejected all formality: he sat down and, glass in hand, launched his autobiography. Round-faced, with knowing eyes, he spoke French with amazing fluency.

"My name is Akoi Guilawogui. Anyway, everybody knows me. I am the finest tailor in the country." Without breaking off, he rose. "If you need a pair of pants, at your service." And with a sweeping gesture he called attention to the impeccable cut of his jodhpurs. Then he sat, leaned forward, and lowered his voice.

"I know why you're here, and I can help you. I'm a candidate for the chief's job in Gueriguerika. My younger brother, who just died, was chief, and I ought to replace him." He took a long swallow. "Over there they already do what I say. I'll put you in touch with the head witch-doctor, and we can work together."

I shook my head.

He went on, persuasively: "You make movies, and I'm a very good actor; you make recordings, and I sing very well, even songs unknown here, because I've traveled a lot. Come with me on my campaign tour."

The way things were, what could we lose by accepting? A few rounds of drinks followed; then he rose and arranged for a meeting in the morning.

"I'll begin at Bofosso," he said. "Tomorrow's Thursday, market day over there; the whole district comes."

Bofosso was on the road from Macenta to Guekedu, not far from Soguru, where the great tattooing ceremony was to take place.

In the morning we met him, as agreed, at a principal intersection of the Guekedu road. We spotted him right away in the crowd, by his nylon hat. A motley crowd was wrestling its way onto trucks, and the trucks were straight out of the junkyard. The native transport lines usually bought them from the European companies when the latter decided they were unfit for further use. On each running-board a hawker stood, shouting the advantages of his vehicle and urging prospective passengers to reserve space immediately; it seemed that space was limited, which was easy to believe, seeing the platforms were loaded with bundles, bicycles, cackling poultry, and a steady flow of new passengers.

"I reserved five places on this one," Akoi announced officiously, pointing to a particularly dilapidated truck. "Your baggage will follow in another. I've taken care of everything."

He introduced us to the driver, one of his friends, and after a painful take-off the adventure began; no one could have called it a "ride," over the forest roads and under those mechanical conditions. On level ground everything was all right, but at the slightest sign of uphill going two apprentices jumped off the truck and ran along behind, carrying huge triangular wedges, which they jammed under the wheels at the first indication of motor fatigue. These apprentices were young boys who did all the driver's dirty work for him; their reward was occasional permission to take in hand the fate of eighty passengers, all of them indifferent to their fate anyway. The memory of our first ride, and perhaps a lack of experience, kept me from sharing their fatalism. At each long, downhill swoop, with the clutch disengaged, I waited, agonized, for the final crash. When the swooping was done with and the agony gone, and I looked around with a deep, peaceful feeling of relief, all I saw was delighted black faces, drunk on speed. To them, these terrifying dives were a happy substitute for roller-coasters.

It took us three hours to cover the twenty-five miles to Bofosso. Allowances had to be made, of course, for stops at every stream to fill the radiator, for the ferry-crossing of the Makona River, and for innumerable expeditions under the hood, conducted by the apprentices, greedy to explore the mysteries of internal combustion.

We came to a halt in the market place. With gratitude for salvation, I jumped off the truck. In big block letters on the rear panel were these words: EMERGENCY EXIT. GOOD LUCK. So the driver had no more illusions than I did about his truck's potentialities.

With no special program, we mingled in the clamoring crowd and wandered among the improvised stalls. Uncountable Diulas, peripatetic merchants, were selling razor blades, condensed milk, suspenders, flowery cotton prints, used tires, sovereign remedies for the greatest variety of illnesses, and an omnium-gatherum of merchandise absolutely useless in the bush. On the largest counters bags of Toma coffee were heaped.

The stink of dried fish drifted through the burning air. Almost everywhere half-naked women waited for customers, seated on the ground, expressionless, before tiny flat baskets containing three measures of red pimento, two handfuls of kola nuts, and half a bunch of bananas.

At the far end of the market place the butcher, helped by his assistants, calmly slaughtered the bull he was about to retail.

———

At night the forest seemed to thicken, to ring the village more closely. We had moved into a small hut across from the *gargote*. This word, brought in by the first white men, was a perfect name for those roadside inns and bars which catered to African truck-drivers and to the eternal day-laborers, constantly repairing roads constantly ruined by storms. The shrill sound of a harmonica and the shuffling of dancers were audible within.

I crossed the road and went into a low-ceilinged, smoky room, where the only illumination came from a couple of lanterns. No women in sight. To an African theme repeated incessantly on the harmonica by one of the dancers, men circled the room in single file, dragging their feet. Wearing turbans, Basque berets, or soft felt hats, they were dressed in ragged European clothes, darned and patched and tattered. One of them puffed away at his pipe while he danced.

Baré, the owner, greeted me with a wide smile. His head was shaved clean and he had a long straggling mustache, and that morning, when we had seen him for the first time, Jean had baptized him "Aladdin." Baré was exhausted. In this one day, because it was Thursday, weekly market day, he had sold, glass by glass, eleven seventy-five-gallon barrels of wine, and his customers were still ordering it: *doboigui,* red wine, the white man's most appreciated contribution to Toma life. He poured me a glass of it, and I sat down on a bench. Through clouds of smoke floating around the lantern hung from the ceiling I watched the dancers.

They went on dancing in a circle, chanting raucously. Every little while the harmonica-player, without breaking rhythm, blew a little louder on his instrument, and the men interrupted their monotone singing to shout sharply. Sometimes one of them left the circle and fetched glasses of doboigui. He held them to the light, checking to see that the levels were equal, and handed them to his friends. Dizzy from the noise and motion, irritated by the smoke, I said good-night to Baré and got out of there.

———

In our hut Virel had brought out his tarot deck, the Marseille tarots. He had been studying symbolism for years, and tonight he explained it all to Tony, who knew very little about it. Virel used the deck to foretell futures, and claimed that he could tell anyone his destiny and character. Tony, skeptical, asked for a demonstration, and Virel dealt out the cards, happy to oblige.

Akoi, candidate for the job of district chief, came in just then, followed by a strange character, tall and thin, very dark-skinned, wearing a very wrinkled, oversized black felt hat and a filthy beige raincoat belted tight at the waist; he had long, untrousered black legs and was barefoot. Popeyed, with a noble, slightly wooden face, he kept his silence in a corner of the hut.

Fascinated by the bright-colored cards, Akoi stood near Virel and listened attentively to his explanations. Akoi could not resist the temptation of prophecy; Tony made way for him at the small table. Both cheerful and worried about the results of his campaign tour, he kept discovering hopeful signs in the tarots. Virel hardly dared contradict him, and they agreed on a compromise: if everything worked out well, he would be district chief.

Akoi got up. Without a word, the man in the raincoat took his place. With his high, bulging forehead forward over the cards, he maintained his silence, but his face betrayed the effort he was making to follow certain slightly ambiguous interpretations. When Virel told him: "The forest is your kingdom," he decided to let us hear the sound of his voice:

"That's true," he said gruffly. "In the forest I walk before all others. I am a witch-doctor."

"See?" Akoi interrupted triumphantly. "I brought you the man you wanted. Fix it up with him. I don't want to get tangled up in this sacred-wood affair. Voiné Koiwogui, and only he, can help you."

Akoi left us. Voiné watched him go, turned back to us, and shrugged. "Better if he keeps out of it. He's not tattooed."

He said that with such quiet scorn that we were all a little embarrassed at not having the obligatory marks.

"And," he added placidly, "he'll never become chief. To be a district chief in Toma country, you have to be something of a witch-doctor or you die very soon. His younger brother—lasted less than two months. . . ."

We started right in explaining to Voiné what we wanted. He had known already, but his intelligent eyes tried to make out our intentions on our faces, regardless of the words. I liked the man. There was a bond between us: he sensed more than he understood. I told him that we wanted to break down the last barriers that remained between white and black, and that to do this we had to know the secrets of the Toma.

Voiné listened to me pensively. A long silence fell over the hut. Big luna moths, coming through the open door, fluttered around the lantern. Outside, in the darkness, the rising murmur of forest insects had almost covered the harmonica's nasal chords.

Voiné rose. "These things are to be learned slowly," he said gravely. "It can't be done in a day. I'll have to think about what you've told me. Good night."

He disappeared into the shadows of the deserted village.

"You think he'll come back?" Tony asked.

"If he's a witch-doctor, he's probably the only man here who can help us."

Virel dimmed the hurricane lamp. We talked it over for a while, lying in our hammocks and smoking cigarettes.

The harmonica was silent.

Suddenly Voiné, draped in a blanket, appeared in the doorway. He came back into the hut as abruptly as he had left. He seemed solemn and decided. He hadn't been able to sleep. White men had never spoken to him that way.

"I'm a pure-blooded Toma," he said. "My name Voiné means 'stubborn'; Koiwogui, my family name, means 'those who do not eat panther,' the true men of the forest. Your skins are not the color of mine, but we shall be like brothers, of the same father and the same mother, and I will show you the secrets of the Toma. I am not afraid of death. Tomorrow, to begin with, I will make a sacrifice to my Spirit; and we'll go together to see the master witch-doctor, Vuriakoli."

The next day Akoi went off alone on his campaign tour, and we set up our base camp in Bofosso.

CHAPTER TWO

We followed Voiné through the forest. The narrow trail twisted among enormous, inextricably interlaced strands of liana. We had been walking for several minutes when Voiné halted to show me an immense tree-trunk; its roots, meshed in a triangular figure, brought to mind the tail of a standing rocket. Out of one of those panels of soft wood a rectangle seemed to have been crudely hacked.

"That's where we get doors for our huts," Voiné said.

The smooth trunks rose nearly a hundred and fifty feet and were lost in a dense arch of leaves. Below, soft light washed over giant ferns. As tall as a man, here and there, rose the striated pyramids of termite communities, like immense stalagmites. Voiné examined them in passing and finally stopped before the highest of these yellowish constructions, this one almost seven feet tall.

With a pickax he chopped into the eastern side of the nest, brightened by the rising sun. He cut through quickly to the galleries and, working with precision, hacked away at the swarming subterranean world, indifferent to the painful bites of the warrior termites crowding across his naked arms and legs. He dug through to the bottom, to a spot directly below the point of the pyramid, thrust his hand into the burrow, and triumphantly brought out a large egg of red earth.

It was the termite queen's sheath. He split it with his knife and showed us a kind of whitish larva about six inches long. It was nothing but an enormous distended womb, from which a tiny black head emerged; the womb contracted and relaxed incessantly in a continual effort to expel eggs. Around it small termites, blinded by the light of day, milled frantically.

"Now," Voiné said, "I've caught the district chief of the nest. I can make my sacrifice to Angbai."

He had carefully closed the doors of his hut; no woman and no stranger, even black, could know his secrets. The hut was in darkness. Voiné lit his lantern, took a bulky parcel from a basket hidden in the corner, and opened the parcel.

Out of the heap of panther- and monkey-skins covering it came Angbai, the bush-devil. It was a large black mask, mouthless, expressionless, and horned. The dim lamplight struck deep reflections from its polished flat planes. Voiné set it in a corner of the hut and lined up all his talismans in front of it: balls of coagulated blood and shells, and a miniature Angbai that he kept always in the slash pocket of his tunic.

With his knife he slit the termite queen's belly; he sprinkled the mask and talismans with the juice that oozed out, crushed the limp, slimy body against Angbai, and began his incantations. He had warned us: we were not to disturb him; we were to ask no questions until the end of the ceremony.

His forearms crossed, his hands open, he bowed and rose before the altar he had erected. By the gleam of lamplight that projected his moving shadow on the wall of the hut, his bulging eyes shone in his ecstatic face.

From the other side of the hut, motionless, we watched him.

CHAPTER THREE

37

Now and then he interrupted his obeisances to shake a tiny bell. Finally he flung the kola nuts, to consult the oracle. They fell crackdown. As a sacrifice, Voiné chewed on the nuts and blew the ground kola meat onto the bush-devil's chin and forehead.

He had told us: "When Angbai is upon me, I am no longer Voiné"; now his voice took on a tragic fullness. He bowed low, slipped beneath the skins of the mask, rose, fell to his knees, and hunched, shaking his head wildly. His incantations changed to bellows. He had become a kind of human beast.

We felt so uneasy witnessing this witchcraft in the stifling darkness of the hut that we slipped away, quietly. Voiné might not even have noticed.

When he came to find us in our hut, his face bore no sign of the trance that had shaken his whole being; its only expression was one of intense satisfaction. Quite freely he supplied all the explanations we demanded. According to him, Angbai was the most powerful avatar of the Afwi, the Supreme Being. He had received Angbai from his father, and would transmit it to one of his own sons.*

"But how does he make his will known to you?"

"By the kola nuts," he said.

The kola tree puts forth a fat bottle-green fruit containing five or six nuts, white or violet; these nuts, about the size of a plum, can be split in two the long way by the simple pressure of a fingernail. To interrogate the Spirit, it was necessary to throw four halves to earth. The Spirit's answer was revealed by their fall. Voiné taught us the different interpretations; at first they seemed very compli-

* See Appendix, I: "To Make a Mask like Angbai."

cated, but actually only one combination out of four was inauspicious, which cut down the chances of an unfavorable response.

"And," he added, "if it comes out badly, you can begin again. But not more than three times."

All superstition seems to be governed by the same laws; we toss coins with the same reservations. The Toma, like others, know how to compromise with destiny.

"Today the kolas worked out well," Voiné said. "I can take you to see old Vuriakoli, head of the witch-doctors across the Makona."

A few days later we were still in Bofosso. Voiné seemed to be in no hurry to translate his plans into action. "We'll have to work slowly," he had said, and we didn't want to hurry him; he was our only hope now. Maybe he was right; the waiting would give us a chance to familiarize ourselves more with the Toma country.

Except for market day, when all the tribes of the region poured in, Bofosso seemed deserted. The villagers worked their *lugans*.* They finished harvesting the coffee, and began to clear land for the coming rice-sowing. Only a few of the very aged sat quietly in the shadows of their huts and watched life go by as they chewed their plugs. Occasionally one of them came to pay us a visit, offered us a few kola nuts, and told us his family history; invariably the family was the most important in the district, even in the whole Toma region, before the whites arrived. Voiné always translated condescendingly, convinced of the undeniable superiority of his own ancestors.

* Cleared areas set aside for farming.

CHAPTER THREE

Every afternoon at five we went down to the river for a bath; on the way we met women in multicolored loincloths, who had finished their laundry and were returning in single file, basins balanced on their heads. In the Hollywoodian atmosphere of a tropical garden, where giant ferns formed luminous arches over rocky fountains, we splashed around in lively streams, showered under cascades, swam under great tunnels of liana. Often Voiné came with us. He disapproved strongly of using soap for baths; to his mind, it was to be reserved strictly for laundry.

"It washes too well," he said. "And if a man is too clean, he can't make children."

For the Toma it was essential to have children, and to have as many as possible.

Voiné owned a hut in Bofosso. For the moment he was living there with a wife and a five-year-old daughter; but his home village was half a day's march into the forest. There he kept the rest of his children, his other wives, and his innumerable relatives.

In the cool night air, village life quickened. Forest sounds swelled louder. Through half-open doors we saw squatting figures around fires within the huts. Bulls lowed, wandering freely among the graves. Occasionally two rams would rush furiously at each other; the natives came to their doorways, interested spectators of these desperate battles. It was one of their favorite distractions of an evening.

We decided to give our tape recorder a maiden run one night. Voiné called together the musicians and alerted the whole village;

he helped us set up the equipment and gave us advice wherever possible, to persuade the others of his importance. Starting up the generator was not easy. A sizable crowd followed that delicate operation attentively. Finally the motor turned over, the lights glowed. An approving murmur rose from the crowd. First we wanted to record a trio of singers: a local tailor and Baré's two bar-boys sang in a strange falsetto, accompanying themselves on a kind of lyre. They did not seem to notice the microphone; Tony, holding it, had to follow them in their wanderings. When the first spool was finished, we played it back.

All the natives gathered in a semicircle around the loudspeaker. When they heard the singers' voices come out of a square box, they showed their bewilderment first by a long silence, then by general laughter. The oldest man in the village hobbled up to us and said, through Voiné: "Now I can die. I have seen the white man's most fantastic machine."

Voiné, so sure of himself a little while before, seemed disappointed. He had spiced the recording with loud remarks of his own, and now, though he listened intently, he was unable to find them in the playback. He did not yet know where he had to be relative to the microphone.

"Good," he said. "The machine remembers well. Still, it forgets things now and then. When you're back in France, it will have to translate. Nobody knows Toma back there." Then, pensively, he added: "If I had a machine like that, I wouldn't show it to just anybody. I'd make people pay to see it."

The idea worked on him. He disappeared into the crowd, came

back after a moment, and handed us a hundred-franc note.

"You see? The village elder thought the same thing. He gave me a hundred francs for the machine; now we have to make the others pay."

Custom requires that no stranger among the Toma refuse a gift, but we dragged Voiné aside, into a hut, and made him promise to drop his project.

"We didn't come here to take money from anybody," I said.

"You keep giving things away, and you never take anything. If you go on like that, you'll be out of luck," Voiné answered sternly.

"But we can't make people pay, just the same. We haven't got a license."

"Ah, well, in that case—" Voiné conceded, giving up.

We had found the decisive argument. Voiné had told us the evening before that his brother-in-law had been fined heavily for opening a *gargote* without that indispensable document; Voiné thought of the license as a kind of talisman.

Our hut looked out on the village square, and sometimes in the morning, without bothering to get up, we watched parleys and trials. Voiné translated everything for us. Often the elders came over to ask our opinion. We witnessed several divorces, common enough here, followed by hot discussions (hot on both sides) of the dowry repayment; and we sat through endless settlements of estates. But today there was a more serious affair. The Diulas, the merchants, lived near the entrance to the village. One of them had been robbed of ten thousand francs. Everyone in the village knew everyone else; a suspect was soon discovered. He was dragged to the square and brought up before the elders, and did what he could to defend himself. In spite of his vehement protests they tied loops of tight, wet rope around both his arms, from wrist to shoulder; the sun would dry the rope quickly, and the contracting loops would cut into his flesh. The man squatted at first, then stood up in pain and danced in a circle, his arms flung wide; he hesitated and looked around for help, but saw only cold eyes and impassive faces. He could not even run away; rolls of lacerated flesh were swelling up between the loops. For fifteen minutes he resisted desperately; then he staggered, collapsed on the ground, confessed, and gave away the hiding-place. The court found the money, gave it back to the plaintiff, and sentenced the thief to pay a fine to each villager for having dishonored the village. Our share was one hundred and fifty francs.

I asked Voiné to clear up a few fine points. "How did you know it was he?"

"It was easy. He had a thief's sacrifice under his tunic, and we found it."

He showed me a ram's horn, a panther's tooth, and a little bell attached to his own tunic. "I wear the sacrifice of a man who has no money but will be a high chief later on."

"A little like an identity card," Jean remarked.

"Absolutely," Voiné answered, using a word he had learned from us; he was impressed by its elegance. "If you can get a look at a Toma's sacrifice, you know immediately just what he wants."

CHAPTER THREE

43

"Why do you call it a sacrifice?" Virel asked.

Voiné told us then that the Toma word "*saragai*" had many meanings. "First of all it means what every Toma, man or woman, always carries with him to show his social rank or his ambitions. It also means all the fetishes that protect; they protect the hut, the family, the village, the totem—like the seven stones in a liana net hung from a wooden bar supported by two upright forks: this guarantees long life to the head of the family. Or the felled sapling that guards each family's plot of land."

Any offering to ancestors or forest spirits was also called "*saragai*"; and, with even more reason, human and animal sacrifices.

While he was lecturing, Voiné told us that the founder of a village always divided the land among the different totems. A Toma tribe is divided into many groups, each with an animal totem. No member of one of these groups, man or woman, can eat the totem animal, or marry another member of the totem. These restrictions are so important to them that they have substituted for the usual "What's your name?" the question: "What animal is it that you don't eat?"

The year before, we had noticed that vegetable totems also existed; Kowo Guilawogui, who did not eat dog, did not touch cassava either. One day he had led me outside the village to show me his sacred plants, so well cared for that they formed a kind of tunnel, in the center of which sacrifices had been heaped up on a flat stone. I wanted to know if that was an isolated case; but explanations of this kind were so tiring to Voiné that he always seized upon the first pretext to interrupt them. Tonight he thought it imperative that he go and prepare dinner.

After dinner he made himself comfortable in the hut, and I asked him to tell us about the sacred wood, about its origin, and about the origin of the first Toma. He didn't seem to understand my questions too well.

"Anyway," I said, "you ought to know how the first man on earth came to exist."

"You'll have to ask Baré about that. He knows better than I."

I shouted to Baré, in his *gargote* across from us. He came over, a wide smile on his face.

I repeated my question. "Baré, do you know the story of the first Toma?"

Without hesitating, Baré launched into the story of Adam and Eve, though he had forgotten their names.

"The first man was alone. He fell asleep under a tree. The Great Spirit came to him, took a piece of him, and made a woman."

He was making obvious efforts not to forget the slightest detail. Even so, when he was through I said: "But that's the story of the first white man."

"Yes," he said simply. "It was American Christians who told me."

Then he said that in Liberia, where he had spent some time, the Protestants had converted him, but that he was no longer accepted now by his coreligionaries. He had sworn not to have more than one wife; and though he had actually had not more than one at a time, he was now up to his fifth since his baptism.

CHAPTER THREE

45

"If a woman's no good, you have to exchange her. The missionaries don't understand that," he finished, distressed at this narrowness of outlook.

But I insisted that they tell me the origins of the first Toma, not of the first white man. Voiné and Baré exchanged perplexed glances.

"Well," Voiné said, "nobody knows. Even the oldest, the blind men with no more hair, couldn't tell you. Their grandfathers didn't live here, and they don't know what went on in the country they came from."

Defeated by this inplacable ignorance, I changed the subject, intending to get back to the question some other time.

———

"You can get your equipment ready," Voiné said, with his habitual smile. "I've found porters. We'll leave this morning for Guiziuma. They're holding a big ceremony there for an elder who died."

He made the announcement in an imperative tone, admitting of no protest. Anyway, all we wanted was to begin shooting.

Voiné had hired not only porters, but also a small tom-tom orchestra. In Toma country important people never travel without music; all through the trip, five men sang our praises, accompanying themselves on little shoulder-slung drums.

"In this country musicians are like women," Voiné decided philosophically. "If you have money they're all around you, telling you you're a great chief."

This was the first time since our arrival at Gueriguerika that we had plunged into the forest. The trail was well kept up, relatively easy, but on either side enormous tangled cables of liana formed two impenetrable curtains. Occasionally we had to cross a stream, wallowing in warm, stinking mud up to our waists.

We came out along a black, deep-running river full of dead trees. A bridge of half-rotten lianas crossed it. We could only cross one by one, and we were worried about the equipment.

"It will have to be rebuilt before the rains," Voiné said. "The devil will take care of it."

He explained that women and non-initiates were given to understand that the devil alone built liana bridges. So the men would have to throw one up from one bank to the other in a single night.

We went through a small village; its inhabitants welcomed us with a great display of friendship, and heaped small gifts upon us. In exchange, I left a small amount of money with the chief, and Voiné gave me a very disapproving frown.

"You should never do that," he said. "When you come to visit them, they're the ones to make gifts. In Toma country it's always like that. Ask me before you do things. I know the customs."

Once more all I could do was defer to his greater knowledge.

A little while before we reached Guiziuma, as we were passing the sacred wood, ferocious screams rose from the bush; the initiates, probably performing some secret rite, were warning us away from the forbidden area. But the whole village was already running out to meet us, and the crowd almost carried us to the central square. Shortly we heard the reason for all this enthusiasm: the man whose death they were mourning that day had been, in his youth, companion to the first white men who explored the country, and we had entered the village—where no foreigner ever came—just as the ceremony was to begin. The coincidence seemed miraculous to them.

The elders, who had invited us to sit, took turns making speeches of welcome, and set the usual gifts at our feet: kola nuts, rice, gun-powder. One almost endless oration succeeded immediately upon another. The owners of guns came to show us their weapons (loaded with blanks), moved away, and fired into the air in our honor. They made these holiday blunderbusses in local forges, using a variety of material, particularly old bicycle frames. They were not the safest of arms; now and then a gun-barrel would explode, shredding the shooter's hands.

An old man approached us with a hundred-franc note in his hand. Voiné resumed his interpreting.

"The old man says he has nothing else. But we can't give money to the whites, because they make it themselves."

After a brief conversation with the old man, Voiné pocketed the bill; he was not white himself.

The hour of sacrifice had come. The victims, a cock, a ram, and a bull, offered up by the dead man's family, were brought into position. It was necessary to honor the memory of the deceased, and to prove to all that he was rich and esteemed.

A witch-doctor began his eulogy; the great funeral drums, like hourglasses upright on the ground, punctuated his phrases. The animals were slaughtered and quartered. The earth soaked up a tide of blood. Only the bull was divided among the spectators. We were given choice cuts: filet, brains, and liver. Musket-shots boomed out from time to time.

Suddenly the women and children scattered in all directions. A gigantic black mask, crowned with feathers, had emerged from the forest: the Bakorogui. His red, gaping mouth opened over his tufted beard; he brandished a devil's trident, symbolizing the dread blow of the panther's claws.

Three musicians escorted him, singing and hammering away with short drumsticks at a kind of hollow iron banana. He crossed the village, dancing anywhere and everywhere, charging at the uneasy spectators. He plunged forward, rocked backward, waved his arms, lowered his head; the variety of gestures was so expressive that the rigid mask itself seemed to show joy, sadness, fury.

He stopped abruptly before a niche next to one of the huts; in the niche was a strange object, a kind of large feather duster the handle of which, covered with clotted blood and encrusted with shells, ended in a sharp blade.

"That's a *simongui*," Voiné told me, "the *gri-gri* * that keeps children from being eaten by the witch-doctors."

The Bakorogui went on with his dance, and accepted an offering at each hut. We asked Voiné to give him ours. Was he trying to thank us? He leaped toward us, threatening, before he disappeared into the near-by forest.

Shots cracked out over a deafening uproar. Whirling clouds of powder and red dust swallowed up the village.

That evening, back in Bofosso, Voiné was in a good mood, very smug: thanks to him we had been able to film those ceremonies.

* Charm or talisman. (Translator's note.)

CHAPTER THREE

49

Unfortunately, what we really wanted was something else again. The year before, we had shot what anyone at all was permitted to see. Now we wanted to penetrate to the great secrets, and we were ready to undergo the rites of initiation. Only Voiné could help us. I reminded him that he was supposed to take us to the master witch-doctor.

Voiné, whose great sensitivity we had always respected, lowered his head, mortified. He seemed to be in deep reflection. Then, out of his meditations, came this surprising declaration:

"Tomorrow we'll go to the mission, to the white fathers, to see Vuriakoli."

FOUR

Deep in the bush, through the middle of a vast cleared area adjacent to the Macenta road, a lane climbed between two lines of flowers toward the large rectangular hut of the Baluma Catholic Mission. To one side a chapel, a school, and an infirmary looked out over the playground. The iron roofs were rusty; a layer of whitewash covered the walls. The architectural style was out of date; the fathers had been in the country for a long time.

En route, Voiné had elaborated his point of view. "I worked for the fathers; I know them. They even wanted to baptize me, but I wouldn't. My father had given me Angbai, and I kept him. A man cannot do two things well at the same time. The fathers are the white man's witch-doctors, and the black man's witch-doctors have taught them many secrets. The fathers have never betrayed them. All the Toma, even Vuriakoli, trust their word. If you promise in their presence not to reveal anything to the women or the non-initiates, the master witch-doctor will share our secrets with you."

The priests welcomed us very cordially. In spite of Lent, they did not hesitate to offer us all that rigorous fasting denied them: tobacco, alcohol, and meat; and we did not resist the temptation to have one good European meal. But how was I to present my request to the father superior? After dinner he guided us around the mission buildings, and I took advantage of the moment to swing the conversation to Voiné, who had not come with us, and to describe our whole project. His face showed the greatest bewilderment; of course, he kept up the most neighborly of relations with the master witch-doctor, but he thought it impossible that we should be granted permission to film the secret rites. In his opinion, Voiné was full of illusions. But when I insisted, he agreed to arrange an interview with Vuriakoli for us.

Voiné left us at dusk, very optimistic. "I'll be back tomorrow morning with the master witch-doctor, and everything will exist completely."

It was the first time he had used that metaphysical phrase, but later on we would find it often in his conversation.

Early in the morning the father superior came into our room. "You may not realize it, but today is Sunday. We'll be saying Mass, but please don't feel obliged to come."

He had saved places for us near the altar. Tony, who was not religious, took pictures, thus saving appearances. Fichter, Virel, and I were surprised to find ourselves singing Mass with the natives, in Latin. We didn't get a word of the sermon, which was in Toma.

Across from us a father was seated at the harmonium. Now and then his instrument sputtered and choked, emitting strangled noises. We exchanged speculative looks. In the end we had trouble keeping straight faces.

The night before, a boy told to clean the harmonium had poured buckets of water over it. The keyboard, warped from one end to the other, and the harmonium's innards were seriously damaged.

· · ·

The bells tolled loudly, and the mission pupils left chapel in single file, their arms crossed, as pious as holy pictures. A man was walking up the flowered lane; we recognized Vuriakoli without ever having seen him. Draped in a sky-blue tunic (extensively patched) and wearing a red turban set well back on his head to reveal three white braids, he bore a devil's trident in his right hand. The children threw him frightened glances and gave him a wide berth.

The father superior felt that this extraordinary interview should be conducted as discreetly as possible; he invited the witch-doctor and us into his office, away from the stares of the curious. Only Voiné and the mission's interpreter were authorized to be with us. The father opened the session, pausing after each sentence to let the interpreter translate. Sullen-eyed, icy-featured, Vuriakoli listened. Not a muscle moved in his ascetic face.

"The whites," the father finished, "promise to reveal nothing to the women and non-initiates. I stand behind that promise; you know me well enough to trust me."

The witch-doctor did not answer immediately. The results of our second attempt might depend on his few moments of reflection. I hardly dared breathe. Across from me Vuriakoli's dark figure stood out against the rectangle of harsh light in the doorway. Vuriakoli never looked at us.

"Last year," he said finally, "two of these whites were allowed to film the Guelemlai and the initiates' departure, in Niogbozu, thanks to my authorization."

Jean and I exchanged a swift glance. Until that moment we had been in ignorance of this detail.

CHAPTER FOUR

Vuriakoli's gruff voice became sharper. "This time they want too much. I do not want to die. I will not teach them anything of the Toma secrets."

Without another word he rose, walked out, and went back down the flowered, sunny lane, beating the air with his trident.

The father superior turned to us with a helpless gesture. "I did what I could, but I knew what his answer would be."

This refusal, after our failure at Niogbozu, confirmed the district commissioner's opinion. We'd never succeed.

We took leave of the white fathers and started sadly back to Bofosso.

We marked time for two weeks. Between Niogbozu and Macenta, between Macenta and Bofosso, we lost days in futile comings and goings. All four of us were slipping into a depression. Only Voiné remained confident.

"Some of them are a lot stronger than Vuriakoli," he said, shrugging. "He's only chief on this side of the Makona." He bowed his head, spread his arms. "But Zézé Sohowogui, my master, makes all others bow before him. We'll go to see him tomorrow. When he has come to know you well, he'll show you our secrets. He is not afraid of dying."

We left the base camp a few hours late. Voiné had trouble getting together the twenty porters we needed to carry all the equipment. Three of them bore precious demijohns of red wine, so dear to the Toma, even in the depths of the bush.

We were almost pleased to plunge back into the stifling shadows of the great forest. Action was restoring some of our optimism. Even so, the trail was very rough. We struggled often up to our waists in the mud of the ever multiplying streams. In spots Voiné stopped to show us hind or panther tracks. The wild beasts were afraid of men and kept out of sight in the forest. Only the professional hunters managed to see them at close range.

The men spelled each other at the head of the column. Occasionally the leader, without even breaking stride, dispatched with one blow of his short machete a red viper, coiled and swaying on the trail.

We came into a mountainous stretch and crossed a series of steep hills. After one last slope, we emerged from the forest onto a vast rocky plateau. Behind us a verdant sea swept to the horizon. An island of giant trees rose out of the plateau, surrounded by huge bare, flat rocks.

Voiné gestured. "That's my village, Fassavoro. There's not much farming; the soil is very poor, and the men go down to Bofosso to work and support their families."

The porters were far behind; we arrived alone with Voiné.

The women, winding heavy skeins on their outflung arms, were stretching long threads of cotton from one hut to another across the square; the threads had been blued in dyes made of forest fruits. The women were not immediately aware of our presence. Suddenly one of them saw us. She cried out piercingly, alerting the whole village; instantly the square swarmed with people. Voiné was superb as the prodigal son. Anyone would have thought he had been away for years. He flitted from group to group, distributed nonchalant greetings, thanks, and felicitations on all sides, and introduced us to the populace as "the four bosses from Paris." They had all heard previously of our marvelous machine "that has memory," of our magnesium flares, of our cameras. By way of demonstration, Voiné asked to be photographed with us and all the members of his family.

They were all in place: the old blind warrior, brandishing his saber, the elders in Sunday go-to-meeting tunic, the ex-infantryman in uniform and at rigid attention, the women and children squatting in front of us. Suddenly Voiné begged us to wait one instant more. He dropped his flattering pose, dashed into a near-by hut, and emerged with a tiny, wrinkled old man, whom he placed beside himself.

"All ready, now? Don't move!" Tony called, in his best banquet-photographer manner.

When the shutter had clicked, the group broke up, and Voiné introduced us to the little old man. "This is my worst nephew."

For Voiné, "worst" meant the very best possible. We were used to his diction; only the nephew's advanced age surprised us. In spite of all our questions, we never managed to work out the exact degree of relationship between Voiné and the old man. We offered the old man a small bottle of rum nevertheless, without consulting Voiné. A toothless smile slit his dissipated face from one ear to the other. But here we could empty every case of gifts we had without running the risk of reproach. Voiné was at home. Nothing was too good for his family.

He had a hut that had once been his home cleaned out and arranged for the night. A procession of his wives brought us our evening meal. A mountain of rice in an enameled basin, and in little earthenware pots a variety of sauces, pimento or palm oil, with scraps of chicken floating in them. The hut was jammed. The whole village wanted to witness this love-feast. The elders, of course, had priority.

All of them commented, with many gestures, on the practicality of our individual plates, spoons, and forks. As usual, I left the rice alone. I had been far too saturated with it during my previous travels.

Voiné, who had been noticing that for several days, seemed worried. "Not hungry, *patron*?"

"Oh, yes. But for me rice is forbidden," I joked.

He broke out laughing.

"We'll have to call you Morowogui" (He-who-does-not-eat-rice).

The astonishing news spread through the crowd and provoked varied reactions. Voiné translated.

"The old men say that if a man is a Morowogui in this country, he dies. There's nothing else to eat. After this day of hard work you ought to take some. Tomorrow you can sacrifice to the rice to ask forgiveness."

I hadn't known that the taboos could be so easily broken.

"A pure Toma should never do it," Voiné said.

We asked him a few more questions. We learned that under exceptional circumstances any man could eat his totem animal, or marry a woman of his totem, which was equivalent to incest. To avoid condemnation by the spirits, he had to repent of his sin through a number of expiatory sacrifices. Any morality, however rigid, is flexible enough to be adapted to life. The Toma in this are no different from the rest of mankind.

Voiné had prepared a surprise for us. A group of little girls, eight or nine years old and considerably awe-struck, wearing loincloths and head-scarves, entered the hut and lined up facing us. On the signal of an older woman, they attacked a song of welcome, in chorus. Their frail, youthful voices, a little off key at first, settled into proper pitch. They accompanied themselves by beating time with maracas. They were too timid to look up at us; a few of them even turned their backs. Behind them, on the wall, the lantern threw great dancing shadows.

The following night we were to meet the grand master of the witch-doctors.

———

A tall hill of black boulders cut off the horizon. Voiné pointed. "We'll go that way, alone."

We let the porters go on first, and then swung off the trail, chopping our way through the bush. The tight network of lianas and thorny shrubs thinned out in spots—the mark of those who had long ago preceded us. Gradually we dropped into a valley. A stream snaked through it; clear waters glistened brightly in the yellow-green shadows.

We climbed again, toward the rocky cliff. The sky was hardly visible. We felt as though we were plodding across the floor of a sea; the lianas hanging from the high leafy arch were like ropes trailing from a sunken wreck.

At the foot of the hill, Voiné explained, was the cave of Vevego, a forebear of Zézé Sohowogui, and the first guide of the white men. His spirit lived above, and Zézé came from time to time to offer sacrifices.

We finally broke out of the ferns and thick shrubbery and found ourselves on a flat boulder at the entrance to the cave. Under a shallow overhang lay gifts to Vevego, like votive offerings: an old rifle dating from the time of the conquest and covered with green mold, lying on a pile of stones beside a few rolled straw mats; bundles of *guinzé;* and earthenware pots full of cassava, rice, and dried pimento.

In a crevice in the boulder, Voiné discovered, as he left the grotto, fetters with which the natives had once been chained for their voyages into slavery. He took this as a good omen; we never knew why. Zézé would help the whites because his ancestor Vevego had done so before him. We climbed to the crest of the hill, and Voiné showed us an immense footprint in the rock. He stepped into it.

"Old Oko walked there when the earth was still soft," he said.

"Who was Oko?"

"Oko was the man who founded Tuwelu, the village of my master Zézé."

On the other side of the valley thatched roofs rose out of the bush. Voiné pointed. "There—that's Tuwelu."

. . .

CHAPTER FOUR

59

Tuwelu differed from the other Toma villages we had been through. The huts almost touched; ancestors' tombs were more numerous, and the headstones higher, than anywhere else. We walked around the freshly turned earth of an open grave; at the bottom we made out the straw mat around the corpse: two spears had been driven through it.

Voiné, questioned, answered: "It was an old witch. She's been dead for three months, but every night she comes back, comes into the huts and sits on people's heads; so they dug her up and nailed her to the ground. That way she keeps still."

The villagers had prepared a hut for us. We strung our hammocks and ate what the women brought to us.

Night seemed to fall very soon.

Voiné entered the hut, followed by the master witch-doctor. The latter was a kind of Buddha, with a shaven head; his features were as icy, his face as impassive, as Vuriakoli's. He wore a dark, dirty tunic.

Wego, the village soothsayer, was with them.

A long silence followed a few remarks of welcome. I made my decision, attacked, and told them quickly who we were and what we wanted. Voiné translated. My last words evoked no echo. Nervously I lit a cigarette. With a brusque gesture, saying nothing, Zézé reached toward the package, plucked out a cigarette; without ceasing to stare at me, he took his time lighting up. He spoke then, in a slow, muffled voice.

"You're in a great hurry," Voiné translated, "and you make your demands too quickly; but that way we know better what you want.

I'll need tonight to think it over. Tomorrow I'll give you my answer."

Zézé stood up, set a handful of kola nuts before us, and left, escorted by his two assistants. Bewildered, we watched them leave. After a few moments Voiné came back, beaming:

"Okay, *patron*; everything's going to exist completely. Look at the kola nuts: all white. That means you're his friends."

I couldn't sleep. Voiné, who was afraid of the dark, like all the natives, asked us not to blow out the lantern; we had simply lowered the flame. The hammocks sketched pale Chinese shadows on a dull, imprecise background. I could hardly make out the figures of my three friends. I was only half aware of the hours slipping by, but I had the impression that I had been wiggling around for a long while, my eyes open, cursing the awkwardness of a hammock.

Suddenly a shout, almost a shriek: "Lights! Lights!"

It was Fichter. I grabbed at the lamp; my hammock dipped toward the ground. I turned up the flame. Virel and Fichter were sitting in their hammocks, with amazed expressions.

"My arm was hanging over the edge," Jean said in an unaccustomed voice. "I felt a cold hand squeezing my own. I grabbed it—when you turned up the lamp I still had it. . . ."

Virel had been shocked awake at the same moment by another cold hand, set on his forehead.

Their hammocks, on different levels, were splayed out from the foot of my own, in opposite directions. Two different beings with cold hands would have had to be wandering around the hut at the

CHAPTER FOUR

same time. It was impossible. I'd have glimpsed at least their shadows.

We decided to leave the solution for morning. I dimmed the lamp. Jean and Virel went back to bed.

This time I managed to fall asleep. But not for long.

A violent jolt knocked me out of my hammock; I found myself standing, without knowing why. Tony was in the same position, as stupefied as I was. Voiné turned up the lamp.

"It's the old woman," he said calmly.

I tried to make him see that those stories were no explanation; anyway, the old woman was nailed down by spears. But it was his story and he stuck to it: "It's completely the old woman, *patron*."

In my own mind these so-called manifestations of an invisible world were not unrelated to our desire to unveil the secrets of the sacred wood. But a logical explanation would never have convinced Voiné; it was better to play the game.

After that active night. Voiné got us out of our hammocks authoritatively. "Zézé will give his answer."

He led us outside the village, to a little clearing where Zézé was waiting, this time in an immaculate white tunic, among the elders. None of them knew a word of French. Once again our fate depended on Voiné, who not only translated, but was obliged to adapt certain phrases to make them conform more closely to Toma rules of politeness.

They all knew what we wanted. During the night they had considered their answer, but Zézé took up the question once more from its very beginnings. He explained how we had come to the village, what he had learned of us from Voiné, and what we wanted of him. Then each of the elders gave his opinion gravely; in general they were favorable. Among the Toma, as with most African tribes, no important affair can be decided without endless palaver. But in the end this custom is nerve-racking. Their decision was made, and I knew it was, and I wished they would get to it.

Finally Zézé turned to us. "The white men," he said, "will have to sign a paper. They will say nothing to the women, to strangers, or to the Bilakoro. They will pay for all sacrifices. Let them wait here a few days and I will have them admitted to the sacred wood. They will hear the voice of the Afwi."

I took out my notebook, wrote the required promise, signed it, and passed it to the others. Tony, who signed last, handed it to Voiné, who translated loudly before turning it over to Zézé.

Zézé stuffed it into a pocket of his tunic without looking at it and rose.

Voiné, stiff and solemn, announced: "The master has agreed to everything. You can go back."

Two or three hours later Voiné, triumphant, joined us in front of our hut.

"You see? Zézé is the greatest of all witch-doctors. He understood that you were not white men like the others."

To simplify the shooting arrangements, I asked him to describe the ceremonies we were to see. But Toma beliefs and reality were so intimately mingled in his mind that we could worm no precise details from him.

CHAPTER FOUR

63

"Zézé blows into the Afwi's head. To do that, he wears his medicine tunic. When you wear that tunic, you can do anything. Zézé becomes very small or very big, whatever he wants. And even if a man is strong, his head spins and he falls, just watching."

Voiné's great ambition was to possess a similar tunic, but the magic garment was very expensive. He ran rapidly through the list of sacrifices necessary to obtain one: Zézé demanded two bulls, seven hundred bundles of *guinzé,* dogs, cocks, and rams. A quick mental addition gave us the total cost, in the neighborhood of ninety thousand francs, or two hundred and fifty dollars. The idea that Toma magic might be the object of such base commerce disappointed us a little.

The day went by far too slowly for us. We tried to kill time by readying all the photographic equipment.

At nightfall, having joined Voiné in front of the hut, we watched women pass, bearing basins of steaming water on their heads.

"Ah," Voiné said, "there go the women with water for you. Follow along with them."

On the outskirts of the village, on wide flat stones, the women set down the basins. Around us in the twilight, on other circles of stones, some sheltered by leafy boughs, groups of naked men and women, squatting, were already washing themselves. With slow gestures they sprinkled themselves, gossiping quietly. In the semi-darkness streaming water glistened on their black skins.

I lingered awhile over the washing, and was the last one back in the hut. I saw at first glance that tonight the table had been set with special care; a rainbow-striped loincloth served as cover, and Tony had concocted a particularly dynamic kind of Martinique punch. A terrified young Toma came in, handed me a big red bush flower, keeping his distance, and ducked away without a word. A little card was pinned to the stem: "WITH LOVE FROM CARINA." I thought I recognized my wife's handwriting. A sudden happiness filled me. For a few seconds I imagined, absurdly, that she would burst into the hut. Then my three friends shouted in chorus: "Happy birthday!" It was true; today was the 10th of March. We had left Paris almost a month before. Virel showed me his notebook and I read: "March 10, don't forget the florist." He was keeping a promise he had made to Carina.

Voiné didn't understand what the noise was all about.

"I'm thirty years old today," I told him.

I saw that the explanation was unsatisfactory. Old Zézé broke in: "How do you know it's today?"

Guinea has its Bureau of Vital Statistics, but in the bush no one ever knew the exact date of a child's birth, and it was often registered several months late.

To enter the sacred wood was the only birthday present I wanted, but there were no indications that any ceremony would take place that night.

"It won't be tonight," Jean said disenchantedly. "With them, you know, nothing is ever urgent."

———

Time dragged the next day. A low, ash-colored sky hung over the bush. The heat was sticky, overwhelming. In the afternoon enormous

CHAPTER FOUR

65

violet clouds wheeled across the leaden sky. They seemed to converge on the village from all points of the compass; yet the air hung heavily still.

Fleeing figures took shelter in the huts. A low murmur rose from the bush. The square was deserted. An instant later a violent gust swept through the village. Whirlwinds of red dust came to life. Lightning slashed through the dark sky. With uninterrupted roars of thunder, a sheet of rain poured down. . . . The huts disappeared behind a liquid wall.

Ten minutes later it was all over. The deep gutters dug between the huts were almost dry. That brief storm, first harbinger of the rainy season, might have been a bad omen to the Toma.

"That does it," Jean said bitterly. "One more reason to postpone tonight's little celebration."

But Voiné was delighted. "Zézé made the rain fall to wash away the poisons in the air. But tonight everything will be dry, and you'll hear the Afwi's voice."

Feverishly we finished our preparations. Voiné remained calm, and left us after dinner, without a word.

The cool air remaining in the storm's wake did nothing to diminish our uneasiness. The village lay wrapped in a heavy silence. We had no desire even to talk. Lying in my hammock, mulling over Voiné's fantastic stories, I had to admit that I was not too cheerful. I had been waiting a whole year for tonight's revelations.

Minutes and hours passed. Voiné had not come back. Doubts assailed me. Could Jean have been right a little while before? Would the Toma postpone the ceremony?

I did not hear Voiné come in. Suddenly he was there, in the middle of the hut.

"Bring your machine and follow me," he said quietly.

We followed him across the deserted square, through the black night, guided only by far-off flickers of lightning that brightened the dark, compact mass of forest before us. We passed the last huts and came to the narrow symbolic gateway. I stopped for a moment. A strange and violent emotion took hold of me, on the sill of this forbidden door. But Voiné gave us no time to savor the long-awaited moment; he plunged ahead, into deep shadow.

Over his shoulder I made out a vague gleam ahead of us. We emerged into a large clearing of tamped earth; its borders were lost in darkness.

The witch-doctors were there, some fifteen of them, standing around a lantern. We knew those men. They had been friendly and companionable. But there was not a gesture, not a word of greeting for us. Eyes lowered, they stared obstinately at the ground. Around us rose the mysterious music of forest insects.

Zézé Sohowogui squatted before an old chest covered with ground kola. He took from it a tunic hardened by the dried blood of sacrifices and encrusted with a rectangle of shining oval shells: his medicine tunic. Voiné's beliefs came to mind; I stiffened involuntarily.

The old witch-doctor's gravity, the solemnity of his gestures, the meditative attitude of the men, indicated clearly that one of the essential rites was about to take place. I wanted to begin shooting, but Voiné, by a simple pressure of his hand on my arm, made me

CHAPTER FOUR

understand that it was still too soon. Zézé stripped completely, donned the sacred tunic, slung over his shoulder two long skin talisman-bags stained brown by blood, and set a kind of fur toque on his head. Then he grasped his trident, and one of his assistants handed him a bulbous black jug.

Very slowly, he raised the jug to his lips. A raucous, savage cry ripped through the dense forest night. Wego, risen from the shadows behind Zézé, roared an answer into an identical pot. The two bellows alternated, the gigantic lowing of antediluvian monsters, an inhuman music of primeval ages, awakening an unspeakable agony in the soul of man. Soon the witch-doctors added the sharp, diabolical tones of their flutes, counterpoint to the two great voices. Voiné signaled that we could begin.

Dazzled for an instant, the men recoiled at the flash of the magnesium flares. They had never seen this before. But the sacred music did not stop: it was the voice of the Great Spirit, and the Afwi was incapable of fear, even before the white man's inventions. The whole clearing surged out of the night, taking on the proportions of a cathedral. Huge trunks rose like columns; heavy branches met overhead like arches.

Behind us, in the village, the women and the Bilakoro must have been lying flat in the darkened huts, terrified by the proximity of the spirits. All around us the forest held its breath; its all-pervading, constant voice was stilled. All life seemed suspended.

The witch-doctors had forgotten our presence and were whirling slowly in the center of the clearing, haggard, lost in ecstasy. They had wrested their magic from the earth, from rocks, from the monstrous vegetation, from the animals of the bush; they were its transmitters, and it passed through them now, shouting man's great primordial fear.

Voiné stared at me almost despairingly, before joining them. "This was the great thing that no white man should see." His voice trembled. "It is no longer a Toma secret."

We had lost all idea of time. Jean shot almost uninterruptedly, and only the number of flares, lit one from another, gave us any notion of minutes passing.

And then, suddenly, the whole company of witch-doctors was marching on us, with an air of defiance, almost of hatred. For a moment they had forgotten the ritual, and we were seeing their true faces, made still more tragic by the brutal lighting.

Zézé, the first, stopped. He seemed to be coming out of a nightmare; he looked at us as though he had never seen us before; his stupor soon gave way to a sadness, a limitless pain. Now he had understood: because of him, the white man held a Toma secret in his accursed machine. The rhythm slowed; the Afwi's cries were less frequent, less harsh. The light of the flare wavered, turned yellow. Zézé looked miserably at me. His shoulders drooped; his body slumped, in an immense lassitude. The flare gave off a last gleam and went out. Night closed around us.

The lanterns' low flame barely brightened the darkness; the forest was still silent. We didn't dare move. Finally I made out Voiné approaching. I knew that I ought to say something, but I felt empty; I wished that I could grasp Zézé's hands, without useless words.

"Tell Zézé—tell him I'll never forget."

CHAPTER FOUR

FIVE

In spite of our daily protests, Voiné persisted in waking us at dawn.
(He loved to speak French. He had volunteered his linguistic
theories with great conviction: "Other languages, they're worthless.
But French, French is a solid language, very gallant.") In his own
noble style, he rephrased his persuasive arguments: "In the time of
the Samori, during the native wars, the great Toma battle-chiefs rose
a little before dawn and took a solid breakfast. They did not speak.
They did not open their doors. When they came out, ready to do
battle before the others were ready, they won victories."

Flattered at being compared to such illustrious personalities, we
had tried timidly to remind our witch-doctor guide that he was
talking about a bygone age; but he would have none of it.

"When white men enter the sacred wood for the first time, it's
like a war."

The next morning, though, he left us to ourselves. After the
sacred music, discussion must have gone on until well along at
night.

When he finally appeared, he told us: "The oldest men in the
village, who know that you want to learn about the Toma, would
like to tell you the story of Tuwelu. When you're ready, come to the
square."

The elders were seated on the largest of the tombs; its black rocks
must have covered twenty square yards. The men watched us approach, in silence. We made ourselves comfortable among them.

THE SACRED FOREST

The oldest villager, wearing an immense gray cowboy hat lined in green, which he had doubtless brought back from Liberia, rose and stepped to the middle of the circle. Voiné translated.

"Oko, ancestor of Zézé, arrived one day from the savanna to the east; he crossed all the Toma country without finding a spot to settle in; then he stepped onto the great black boulder across the valley, but in those days the earth was still soft, and the mark of his foot has remained in the stone."

The old man stopped and turned to his neighbors. He bowed his head, and all, in chorus, pronounced the sacramental *"Egow!* (It is true!)"

"He decided to found a village near the rock. His wife and brother-in-law helped him. When the hut was finished, lightning destroyed it, and he came here, to the place that is now Tuwelu, the place where there are many kolas." *

"Egow!" approved the elders in one voice.

He went on with his story:

Much later, when the white man penetrated Toma country, the people of the village, after trying to hold off the whites by force of arms, and becoming convinced that the effort was futile, joined them as allies. Two men, Vevego and Bagvila, ancestors of the present chiefs, agreed to serve as guides for the whites. Kowo, a great war-chief in the region of Bofosso, decided to lay an ambush for them and to wipe them out. But old Kréan, of Doezia, the high chief of the Toma, prohibited this. "If you think you can defeat the white man," he said, "go on with the war alone; he is too strong for us, and

* See Appendix, II: "The Meaning of Place-names."

we prefer to make peace. I will defend Vevego and Bagvila against you." Kowo, furious, attacked the whites, who used cannon against him (a weapon unknown up to that time), and his defeat was so complete that he had to flee, all alone, to Liberia.*

Children had drawn near our group and were listening, motionless, with solemn eyes, to this story they all knew by heart.

The patriarch finished his oration:

"The names of Vevego and Bagvila stand in Toma history with those of the first French soldiers who conquered the country; and you, who have been the first to enter the sacred wood, your names will stand forever with those of Zézé, Wego, and Voiné."

Zézé rose in his turn. "In the days of force † a column of infantry came to the village; its commander sent for the witch-doctor, and I appeared before him. He had me bound by his men and given fifty lashes. I never knew why. For a long time I was unable to walk."

"*Egow!*" chorused the elders approvingly.

"Now you have come, and no white men have ever spoken to me as you have; no white men have ever accepted an invitation to my hut to eat with me, as you have. I understand now that times have changed; so I have revealed our secrets to you. I am no longer afraid of death. Now you may stay in Tuwelu. You are at home here."

All the elders rose and came to shake hands with us, in Toma

---

* See Appendix, III: "The Story of Old Kréan."
† The period during which the whole region was subject to military authority.

fashion, slapping our palms lightly; then they withdrew to their huts.

———

That night, I tried to reconstruct all the details of the previous evening. A memory, at first very vague, came into my mind: a small Indian village, on the banks of a lagoon on the upper Orinoco. There, too, at nightfall the blast of great bark horns terrified the women and children, who cowered out of sight while the men danced around the large tribal hut and called up the voices of bush spirits.

An even more recent memory came to me: the year before, among the Nalu, in the islands of mud and mangrove along the Guinea coast, on a moonless night, I was awakened violently by a furious uproar, a witches' Sabbath. I wanted to go outside; but our guide, sitting in darkness at the doorsill, held me back: "You're not supposed to see that. It's just the men, scaring the Bilakoro."

In most phenomena of the sensate world, sounds play an essential role. At times a door creaking in the night, a shutter flapping, the whistling of the wind, are more frightening than the sight of a real danger. But isn't it due to some deep sense of magic that ritual sounds persist among contemporary primitives?

Wego had closed the door of the hut against the night, against the forest. Deep in my meditations, I had not heard the three men come in. In the shadows all I could see of Zézé was his shining eyes fixed on me.

Voiné, leaning across the lantern, spoke softly: "The old man has been thinking all day, and has told me this: 'The white men have heard the voice of the Afwi; later on they will pass the second obstacle with me and will see the Great Spirit. Now they must learn the secrets of the bush, and Voiné will be their guide; I am too old to follow them, but if they call me, I will come.'

"Tomorrow," Voiné finished, "I'll take you to Sagpaou, the land of the witch-doctors, and you can film men changed to stone by a single cry of the devil."

———

Since our arrival in Tuwelu I had been suffering from an infected chigger-bite in my right foot. Ready to leave now, I noticed that my heel had taken on disquieting proportions. I would have to leave for Macenta immediately. Voiné and the others would go on to Sagpaou in two or three days. I would join them there as soon as possible.

Helped along by Virel, I limped back over the twenty miles to Bofosso. A native trucker took me on to Macenta. After a few days in the hospital, where a military surgeon lanced my abscess, I was in condition to walk; but I could not work my foot into a sandal.

Tony came to meet me at Bofosso, and we struck out directly for the village of petrified men. The trail was rough on my bare foot, and crossing muddy streams made it necessary to change my dressings often. At each village we took a short break, and were welcomed in the usual manner by the natives. In one of them the elders showed us a large bronze bell, hung from the ceiling of the guest hut and bearing a relief of Saint George slaying the dragon. Two women had found it, on their way to do the laundry. How long had it been in the stream-bed? How had it come to be there? No one knew.

"The devil hid it in the stream," said one of the rare villagers to know a few words of French.

The road twisted up the hillside. A faraway beat of tom-toms vibrated on the burning air. On the hill across from us trees were falling with brittle snaps. To the rhythm of the tom-toms, the Toma were clearing a patch of bush, for the imminent rice-sowing.

Bad news awaited us at Sagpaou: Voiné and my friends had just spent another day arguing with the elders, who claimed that they had never heard the legend of petrified men. How could they map out the route to a place the name of which no one knew?

"But I know it," Voiné answered quickly. "It's Banazu."

The elders exchanged shocked glances. Banazu was a secret name, known only to witch-doctors; and Zézé had arranged, a little regretfully, to let it slip. But they went on maintaining their ignorance, and in the face of their stubbornness we dropped the subject temporarily.

Our quarters were in a vast oval hut, a *garopele*, Voiné explained, the hut of a high dignitary. Above the doorway, outside, a small fetish bow and a sheaf of *guinzé* were hung. Against the wall, in a corner, stood an iron-tipped spear, much like those we had seen driven through the witch's body.

To the rear of the hut a notched shaft rose to the attic, a platform set up under the conical roof, where the Toma piled reserves of rice and gourds full of palm oil.

After our meal we strung our hammocks in a zigzag pattern, Tony his opposite the doorway, and Jean his at the rear of the hut. Between Virel and me, on a platform of tamped earth against the wall near the doorway, Voiné spread his mat.

He dimmed the lamp and rolled up in his blanket.

I was very nervous that night. My injured heel throbbed, and I was casting about desperately for some way to bring the witch-doctors around. These petrified men intrigued me. I had already stopped suddenly, near the entrance to Sagpaou, at the sight of polished menhirs of black stone. One of them particularly, split down the middle like an enormous egg, had impressed me. According to Voiné, the trees and lianas were so choked in the forest outside Sagpaou that a man could not make headway without a machete. A very long time before, the men of a now vanished village were dancing and singing to tom-toms, in spite of the spirits' prohibition. The Afwi had shouted a mighty shout, so terrible that the men were petrified on the spot.

Here in the heart of the bush, then, there was a chance that we would stumble on the remains of a megalithic civilization, as on Easter Island. All the more reason to convince Sagpaou's elders that they must help us.

A light rustling overhead interrupted my thoughts. I stared at the ceiling mats, laid across a frail scaffolding of thin poles. Nothing moved. I forced myself to disregard the sound—a drawn-out scraping of palm leaves.

"If I weren't so tired," Jean said, at my left, "I'd go out there to see what is happening."

Silence answered him.

"I suppose it's only rats," he added, as if to cheer himself up.

From his tone of voice, I gathered that he believed it no more than I did. I made no answer. Gradually the rustling became sharper, more insistent; a dull anguish invaded me: the sensation that an invisible presence, too great for the hut, was slipping inside it, filling it, would split it wide open, was straining its whole framework. Out of the corner of my eye I watched the others. They were all asleep, or at least seemed so. My uneasiness grew. I wished that I could attribute it to an attack of fever, caused by the abscess; but I was entirely clear-headed; I was simply tired and stiff. Across from me, Voiné lay asleep.

The rustling died. With an effort, I closed my eyes and tried to doze off.

Suddenly the scraping began again, much more violently; and the door opened with a sharp creak.

Voiné stood on the doorsill, bareheaded, in his short tunic and a pair of bush shorts. But he was there, at my feet, stretched out on his mat. He was lying on his side, his back to me. I saw his shaven nape. The lantern, turned low, was on the ground between us. I was afraid to move. I held my breath and watched him in the doorway. He hesitated for a moment, ducked under Tony's and Virel's hammocks, and slowly dropped to earth within himself.

The whole scene had taken only a few seconds.

I had no idea how much time had gone by when Jean's choked voice roused me from my stupor:

"Did you hear anything?"

"Yes. The door creaked."

But I had no wish to say anything more, or to admit my hallucination.

Tony must have been awake, too. A moment later he got up, in his underwear, left the hut—and came back almost immediately. I had the impression that he was very pale. I rose to one elbow and reached out to Virel's hammock. Virel was in a deep sleep.

The scraping subsided. In the hut, tension dropped; but I lay wide awake and jumpy all night, and fell asleep only in the first glimmering light of dawn.

The next morning no one spoke of the night's events. We even avoided mention of the scraping and rustling. Alone with him for a moment, I asked Voiné: "Did you go out last night?"

"Yes," he said.

An ironic smile, hardly perceptible, drifted across his lips.

The next day, after another palaver, the village elders were a little more understanding. They agreed to give us a guide and a five-man escort. The guide didn't know the exact spot, but claimed he could find it easily.

A couple of miles outside Sagpaou, we came out into tall savanna. The guide stopped to check his landmarks. Above the grass he pointed out a high hill, covered with dense forest. "There, that's Banazu."

Two men broke trail through the brambles and thorns, and we slogged along behind them through the narrow tunnel, which went up and down ceaselessly through the heart of a nightmarish vegetation, as though we were playing at explorers. That little expedition through apparently virgin forest delighted us, filled us with enthusiasm. I had almost forgotten my bare foot and my hardly closed wound.

After several hours of hiking I felt a good deal less optimistic. I hurried to make up the considerable distance between me and the others. Among the trees in a hollow between two hills, enormous rocks were piled pell-mell.

"There it is," the guide said.

Vainly we examined the chaos for some line suggesting human form. We clambered over boulders, investigating everything from all angles; but with the best will in the world it was impossible to pick out even one rock that might justify the anthropomorphic legend Voiné had narrated.

"Maybe the Toma go for abstract art," Virel suggested.

Voiné missed the point of the joke. Furious, he lashed out at our escort, who, with disconsolate grimaces, gestured, machetes in hand, trying to convince him of their good faith.

Then Voiné turned to us. "Nothing here resembles a man dancing or beating a tom-tom," he said sternly. "They want to fool us, but they won't make fun of white men. I've ordered them to take us to Banazu."

All day we wandered through the forest, looking for men of stone. Several times we found rocks that the guide tried, without success, to pass off as the vanished victims of celestial wrath. Voiné was beside himself at this obvious betrayal.

We were hardly back in Sagpaou when he filled the village with

CHAPTER FIVE

invective. The elders, roused by all the noise, hurried out of their huts and assembled in the square.

"This man," Voiné said, pointing to the guide, "has deceived the white men, and made them wander through the bush all day for nothing. He must pay a fine."

This demand seemed fairly useless, but we had no time to intervene: Voiné's protests were so violent that he won his case almost immediately. The elders conferred among themselves, and the poor guide found himself sentenced to pay us two hundred francs in reparations, and a heavy fine to the village for having "dishonored" it, to use Voiné's expression.

I never understood the jury's verdict: the poor man had only done what the elders had told him to; he hadn't led us around all day for his own pleasure. Convinced that they were making fools of us, we asked Voiné about it. He avoided answering directly and advised us to send a runner to Tuwelu to ask Zézé to join us here.

If all went well, he'd be along the next morning. We retired to our hut, and after a quick dinner fell asleep almost immediately, exhausted by our trek through the bush. In the middle of the night I woke, startled by the creaking door.

Zézé walked in, wearing a full, bright-red tunic and a brand-new pith helmet. His features drawn by fatigue and worry, he sat down next to Voiné, on the mat; Voiné sat up, not surprised in the least.

"Thank the old man for having come so quickly," I told him.

"Why? Witch-doctors prefer to travel at night. . . . They're not afraid of bush animals."

Zézé went on at great length in a quiet voice; Voiné nodded and looked more and more worried. I hesitated to interrupt them. Finally our witch-doctor adviser turned back to us.

According to his explanation, the men of Tuwelu had sworn secrecy: no Toma outside their own group would ever know that we had seen the Afwi. But when we had left, one of them had let the story leak to his relatives in a near-by village. Now the whole district knew, and they were demanding that the guilty be punished. The affair could easily develop serious proportions. Zézé asked us not to be too demanding with the elders of Sagpaou, and to go on back to Tuwelu as soon as possible. At Doezia in a few days an assembly of the elders and witch-doctors of the Gueriguerika district was to take place. Our case and the case of our friends would probably be judged. We would have to appear with them, and he advised us to go beforehand to see the man who would preside over the debates: Mamady Guilawogui, the district chief, a former infantryman, who, with a little good diplomacy, would certainly become our ally.

"You'll have to send him a note to let him know you're coming," Voiné said.

I took a dim view of the usefulness of this letter, addressed to a Toma who would probably be unable to read it. But Voiné insisted, and we soon saw that he attributed extraordinary powers to any slip of paper covered with writing; by this means the white man conducted all his affairs and obtained what he wanted; so to Voiné the paper itself was possessed of magic virtues. Which was why the witch-doctors had insisted on a written contract from us.

<hr>

The porters were far behind. We were in no hurry. Our guide estimated that we would be at Mamady's hut within an hour. We took a break on the bank of a stream, in the high grass, to catch our breath and to drink; Voiné, still impatient, went on ahead. Now, alone in the bush for once, we felt free to compare notes.

"Remember that night in Sagpaou?" Jean said to me.

For almost a week now the memory of that night had haunted me; and without knowing exactly why, I had not wanted to talk about it. I let Jean reminisce first. He had seen exactly what I saw. As for Tony, who had witnessed the identical scene, he had topped it: once outside the hut, he had seen Voiné again; but Voiné had just slipped back into his double under our very eyes.

There was no rational explanation for this phenomenon of collective hallucination. Virel, the only one of us completely at ease in the world of spiritualism, was also the only one to have slept peacefully through the whole night. He found our supernatural adventure almost trite.

Jean was sure that the Toma had slipped hypnotic herbs into our food. But we had all had the same hallucination; herbs could not explain that. Tony and I limited ourselves to setting down the facts. But we were all aware that the three nights of sorcery coincided with events of great importance to the expedition.

One last question remained unanswered: why had we all waited so long to talk about the threefold mystery?

———

Mamady was out inspecting his crops. The elders of his village invited us to relax in his hut, while a runner went to report to him.

"Mamady is the richest man in the district," Voiné had told us, "and the commander at Macenta put him in charge of the Gueriguerika until a new chief is nominated."

In the hut an iron garden-chair and a runner of Scotch plaid testified to the owner's highly civilized tastes. Harnesses were hung on the walls. Mamady owned a horse—an exceptional luxury in Toma country. A military good-conduct citation and an active-duty card, in a gold-plated frame, occupied the place of honor.

One after another the men of the village came to greet us and made themselves at home beside us. There was hardly room for Mamady when he arrived, out of breath and sweating; wearing leggings and tennis sneakers, he was tall and potbellied in his full tunic. His pasty, shining face radiated prosperity; but his uneasy eyes rolled, and his hands trembled nervously. For him, "white man" must have been a synonym for "annoying complication."

We reassured him immediately: we were not interested in taxes, nor in administrative affairs, but had come only to greet him as friends. He relaxed, honored us with a wide smile, issured orders in a clipped voice, and a few minutes later led us into a magnificent hut, brand-new, where our baggage awaited us, lined up in impeccable order.

Mamady spoke French fluently. In the hut we managed to isolate ourselves with him and Voiné and got right down to business. From his whole attitude we had understood that it would be useless to beat around the bush with him. He had heard of us and wanted only to throw the weight of his prestige behind us, within the limits imposed by his position. But he had no desire to interfere in the affairs of witch-doctors; he asserted that he had no authority over them, and refused to commit himself on the subject. We pressed him half-heartedly. He gestured nervously, lost his joviality, shook his head with an absent air.

To break off the interview, now become unpleasant, he proposed a tour of his village, and rose. We followed him listlessly. He had already swung back into his merry mood, and repeated to us in all tones of voice that he had never before run across white men like us; he introduced us, in passing, to several of his fifty wives.

Then he led us toward an immaculate white hut where his favorite lived alone. The others were packed five and six to a cylindrical hut.

"My best wife!" Mamady announced proudly.

She was as plump as he was round. This attribute alone, in Toma country, bespeaks opulence. She received us graciously, her hand outstretched.

Her hut was furnished with a genuine spring-mattress bed; illustrated magazines lay in heaps on it. Bright-striped lengths of cloth were on display everywhere. We seated ourselves on the soft bed. Mamady's wife sat on a tabouret across from us. She knew not a word of our language, and Mamady had no intention of interpreting. The conversation consisted in an exchange of smiles.

Distractedly Tony leafed through a magazine.

"Oh, take them along," Mamady said, with a handsome gesture. "They're old, I've read them all."

We rose and took leave of the lady. Tony, starved for literature, had slipped a pile of magazines under his arm. Mamady's wife smiled at us once more. She was the favorite wife of a *grand seigneur*, and she knew it.

Mamady was radiant. In a burst of enthusiasm he offered us a ram, and sent all his available wives fishing. They were to bring back their catch for the evening meal. We went along with them, planning to bathe.

They carried conical nets, something like large shrimp-nets. We were sure that the thirty or thirty-five women, with those contraptions, would barely manage to round up a decent appetizer for us.

The stream, narrow and shallow, snaked along between two curtains of tall grass. Some of the women lined up downstream to make a dam; the others, waist-deep in water, waded toward them, scraping the banks and bed with their nets. Then they began again, a little farther down, until the four of us, splashing in the quick-running stream, lost sight of them.

We had had a fine blowout on Mamady's ram, and now we were replete and sluggish. Mamady and his best wife, with some of the elders, had dropped in afterward. We concocted a punch for them. Mamady kept saying: "Very good! Very good!" in polite tones, but his chubby face contracted into fearful grimaces. He probably failed to understand how anyone could spoil a delectable liquid like rum by adding lemon to it. But he enjoyed our doboigui and made us promise to send him several demijohns of it.

The women were returning from the river. It was deep night now. One of them came to set before us a large basin full of black catfish and went away again. We had no desire at all for a second dinner, but had to be resolutely courteous, so as not to offend our host.

"Four catfish will be plenty for us," I said. "Keep the others yourselves."

No one moved. The basin was there in front of us; the fish, most of them still alive, thrashed around in their last agonies.

"Be better to cook them right away," Jean remarked.

All present kept silence.

Then Voiné said: "We, the Toma, can neither kill nor eat the black fish. They were brought to you alive; if you don't mind, cook them yourselves."

"You know that we have tried to be like the Toma in all ways. Have the women take the fish back to the river."

A murmur of general satisfaction greeted this decision, and the elders told Voiné to transmit their thanks to us.

One of Mamady's many wives came to take the fish. Following a child who carried a lantern, she went back along the trail to the stream; on her head, in the basin now full of fresh water, the catfish were beginning to come out of their asphyxia.

We had escaped the torture of a second dinner, and had made several friends into the bargain. I had thought that only the Zumanigui—those-who-do-not-eat-catfish—were obliged to respect that taboo. Voiné broke into confused explanations, and we learned that occasionally a family, or even a whole region, observed special taboos.

The next morning we said good-by to Mamady. He himself left the village on his white horse. He was off to collect taxes. The night before, he had promised to plead our cause in person at Doezia, but had been reluctant to make any guarantees. On the other hand, he had assured us warmly and endlessly of his unwavering friendship.

———

Even at first glance, Doezia seemed to be one of the key villages of the Toma country. White huts, decorated with huge paintings in black, and grouped around several small squares, formed almost separate villages, terraced up the hillside and hemmed in by dense forest.

We got a fairly cool welcome. Probably the inhabitants had already heard of our sacrilege at Tuwelu. A former infantryman offered us his hut anyway, and the usual parade of dignitaries began. In each handful of kola nuts we found the inevitable white one, token of friendship; but Voiné translated their words of welcome reluctantly. An antagonism had sprung up immediately between the elders and our witch-doctor guide.

In that hostile atmosphere, and tired as we were after the trek, we had not even enough courage to talk things over with them, and we made our preparations for the night very ostentatiously.

They had barely left when an ear-splitting clamor pulled us out of our hammocks. Voiné listened for a moment, and calmed us down: "It's only an old woman dying."

The wailing redoubled; it drowned out the night sounds of the forest. We gave up all hope of sleeping. Until dawn the mourners spelled each other in the darkness of the next hut.

The situation seemed no more favorable the next morning. Flee-

CHAPTER FIVE

ing the painfully hostile atmosphere, we strolled out of the village with Voiné. Near the gateway to the sacred wood stretched a wide esplanade, shaded by gigantic silk-cotton trees. Their trunks at the base must have been forty or forty-five feet around; they were the oldest, the most majestic, that we had seen. The great Toma assemblies, at which were made all important decisions in the Gueriguerika district, took place here.

Forced inaction weighed heavily on us; to pass the time we decided to take a closer look at the wall-painting on the huts. We had seen wall-paintings here and there in other villages, but here we were struck by their number and variety. To them, as much as to the layout of the huts, Doezia owed its special, almost unique character.

They were done in paint mixed on a cow-dung base, and were all the same color, a brownish black, but no two of them were alike. Their ample, elegantly drawn lines suggested no precise figures, unless perhaps vaguely vegetable forms, akin to the supple lotuses of Egyptian frescoes.

In one corner of the village we stopped, fascinated. Standing on a low platform of earth that surrounded a recently whitewashed hut, a very young girl, slender and graceful, was brushing long curves on the wall with a sure, continuous stroke. She stopped to dip her primitive brush in a gourd she held.

"Ask her what she's drawing," I told Voiné.

Voiné stepped closer to her. The girl turned, smiling, and answered in a soft voice.

"She doesn't know," Voiné said. "She paints what's in her head."

"Could you do as well?"

"No. Toma men don't know how to paint. Only their women."

We stood watching for a moment, to follow the design to completion.

"Virel would say it was abstract art," Jean offered.

"No," Voiné cut in; he was still not sure of the exact meaning of that phrase. "It's to make things pretty, and to make the huts more solid. If the women were more intelligent, they would know how to paint panthers on the walls."

Children, seated on the stones of an ancestral tomb, were peeking one by one into a small rectangular box. We came up to them quietly, not wanting to startle them, and asked them for a look at their toy. One of them handed it to us with a smile and a lively gesture. It was a stereoscope, probably brought back as a souvenir by some soldier, and in which they were admiring the Marseille opera house, in colors, in relief, and wrong way up. Without correcting the double image, Jean fell into a deep study of it.

"They're right," he said. "It's a lot better that way."

We had noticed a much smaller hut, not far from our own, that contained, according to Voiné, all the talismans of the village, notably the one that protected it from lightning. At Doezia the natives, for some reason, are terrified by fire; it is even forbidden to light one outside a hut for cooking, unless it is done outside the circle of lianas.

Voiné, possibly as a challenge, decided to cook a meal outside

CHAPTER FIVE

89

the door and took out a few glowing brands. Several dignitaries exchanged comments, seated at their own doorways. Up to then they had been quite pleased to ignore us. As the first spirals of smoke arose, they arrived in a delegation. They sketched ample gestures skyward, and heaped Voiné with vehement reproaches. "You'll bring lightning down on us."

The sky, from one horizon to the other, was of a deep, immutable blue.

A few hours later, with no warning at all, sudden gusts of wind shook the forest, and heavy black clouds unfurled over the bush. Almost immediately the storm came down on the village. We were seated under the awning in front of our hut. None of us had paid any attention to the witch-doctors' threats. And yet a vague presentiment struck us—only a few seconds before lightning did.

The burst of flame was of an extraordinary power. Jean, flung to the ground, dragged Tony down with him. An enormous wreath of fire had blasted into the red earth only a few yards from us.

The clouds of dust dissolved. All the Toma came running up, worried and mocking at the same time. Badly shaken, we tried to restore our prestige: the witch-doctors of Doezia had called lightning down upon us, as they had said they would, but none of us had been hit—so we were still the stronger. They did not seem convinced. Soon a brisk rain dispersed the crowd.

We were almost ready to believe that the witch-doctors had just administered striking proof of their magical powers. But another hypothesis seemed more logical to us: these men lived in permanent contact with nature, and their senses were constantly alert. They had been able to feel the approach of a storm. That morning, when Voiné had violated the village laws, they had been unable to pass up a chance to threaten us with ineluctable punishment. That version of the incident, maybe a little far-fetched, satisfied us for the moment. It might also explain the proximity of the talisman hut—it was certainly not the first time that lightning had struck that spot.

Sheets of rain swept across the deserted square. Between mutterings of thunder, snatches of a monotone chant and the beat of hammering feet came to us from the huts downhill and then drew nearer. The whole village seemed to be climbing toward us.

Terrified goats burst out of an alley between two huts and bounded across the square to shelter. An amazing procession appeared at their heels. Under the driving rain men and women, most of them almost naked, in close-ranked columns, were protecting themselves from the storm by various means: wide conical hats in Indochinese style, basins or bowls upside down, old military ponchos. Even a faded umbrella waved above the parade. The crowd repeated the same phrase tirelessly, beating time to it with their heels.

Among them we recognized Voiné, huddled in his raincoat. "The old woman's funeral is beginning," he said as he passed us.

Later on he translated the litany for us: "The old woman took good care of us . . . the old woman took good care of us. . . ." The cortege was animated by a curious mixture of joy and affliction.

A scudding wind had driven off the last clouds. The only remnants of the storm were wide puddles of water, dazzling in the sunlight.

An orchestra of maracas, composed of ten or twelve women, took its position in front of the dead woman's hut. One after another the old women of the family, mummies torn out of their wrappings, faces covered with earth, hair bristling in all directions as a sign of mourning, executed the funeral dances to the slow, syncopated rhythm of the gourds. Arms outstretched, disjointed, they mimed grief and danced in a circle. Then some of them entered the hut, to reappear bent under the weight of the corpse, which had been rolled in matting. In the rattle of maracas, screams of frantic joy mingled with loud lamentation.

The women set down the body near the grave, a simple hole dug in the middle of the village. Then two or three of them took hold of a small girl about twelve, a relative of the dead woman; the child, haloed by a thick head of frizzy hair, shouted wildly, desperately, and fought with all her strength. The women draped her in a white cotton shroud, laid her on the corpse, held her there by force for several seconds, and then let her run off, disheveled, screaming in terror all the way through the village.

With an effort the women lowered the corpse into the ditch; they heaped on it all that it might need in the beyond: loincloths, food, matting; then, with their hands, they shoveled red earth into the hole until it was full.

Voiné, accustomed to this performance, did not understand why we had filmed it. One thing alone preoccupied him: the assembly, decisive for all of us, that would take place the next day.

SIX

Elders and witch-doctors, preceded by their chair-bearers, had been coming into Doezia from all corners of the district since early morning. They never traveled without those small carved chairs, insignia of their prerogatives, handed down from father to son.

As they entered the village they scattered, to make themselves as comfortable as possible in the huts of their relatives. It would be unheard of for a Toma not to find relatives in any village. And the laws of hospitality were sacred. With interminable assurances of friendship, Voiné welcomed all those who came to greet us; no possible ally could be neglected.

Toward noon Mamady Guilawogui, still in his Basque beret and leggings, made a solemn entry on his white horse, at a slow walk. Beside him walked his best wife. Behind were four or five auxiliary wives. He left his horse to a boy. The Toma had borrowed this word from the whites,* but had dignified it. For them, the "boy" was invested with important functions. Mamady's (one of his "worst" nephews) was a kind of chamberlain.

After chatting with us for a moment, jovial and pompous, Mamady went on toward the long esplanade, to open the session.

We stayed in our hut, to convince them that we had no wish to influence their deliberations. The assembly had been convoked primarily to designate candidates for district chief, and our own prob-

---

* Throughout the colonial world, "boy" is used for waiters, porters, houseboys, and servants generally. With this meaning it has passed unaltered into the French language. (Translator's note.)

THE SACRED FOREST

lem would be discussed as a secondary item. We would have no opportunity to defend our cause; when the witch-doctors called us up, their decision would have been made.

Time passed very slowly. The whole adventure was being reduced to nerve warfare.

In the square, across from us, a Diula had come to set up shop in front of a hut. His merchandise was spread out on the ground on mats, or hung under the thatch awning.

Sitting in our doorway, we waited.

A slender young woman in a striped loincloth passed back and forth in front of us. She was a Malinké, a good deal more attractive than most Toma women. We watched her comings and goings in spite of ourselves. Across the way the Diula kept an eye on us. She was one of his wives, amusing herself by playing the temptress for us.

After a while the Diula crossed the square and joined us. He knew that we had miraculous medicines, and wanted something for his eyes. We treated him with ordinary eye-drops, and he went away very happy.

Toward the end of the afternoon (and with relief) we saw Voiné coming. The witch-doctors had ordered him to bring us to them. On the way he gave us a quick outline of proper conduct. We were to admit that we knew secrets and to promise, once more, that we would never reveal them.

Long skeins of mist hung high in the silk-cotton trees. The sun was setting. In a milky, aquarium-like light, eighty witch-doctors were waiting for us, seated in a semicircle on the esplanade. Mamady, presiding, rose, stepped toward us, and asked me to explain to the assembly what it was that we wanted. The official district interpreter would translate my words faithfully.

Standing within the semicircle, I repeated what I had already told Voiné and Zézé: we wanted to come to know the Toma by sharing their lives, in order to understand them and if necessary be able to help them. Already one of their greatest witch-doctors had allowed us to enter the sacred wood; if they saw sacrilege in that incident, we were prepared to pay the established fines and to undergo the expiation required by ancestral law. We had never used force, and in any case we had no arms, not even a machete, indispensable for traveling through the bush. Nor did we wish to trick them in any way; we would film only what the Toma authorized us to film. If they wished, we would renew for them in writing the agreement we had signed for Zézé.

My speech ended, I went to sit down outside the semicircle, under a tree with my friends.

One by one the elders took the floor. Some favored us and turned to us from time to time, smiling; others, indignant, ignored us. One of them particularly, a little deformed gnome who paced back and forth with jerky strides, exhaled rage as he played drum-major with a striped umbrella-handle. But at twilight there was still no decision. As always when an affair was important, the Toma wanted to sleep on it.

All evening our hut was invaded by elders, who questioned us about Paris, about France. What they wanted most was to hear repetition, and therefore confirmation, of the stories brought back

CHAPTER SIX

95

by their demobilized compatriots. With abundant gestures, we worked out points of comparison. The subway fascinated them. Certain soldiers from the region had stepped aboard subway cars in the morning and emerged only when the last train had gone to the barns. We described a kind of Conakry-Kankan railway line, but faster and underground. Modern buildings and the Eiffel Tower (superposed huts, or silk-cotton trees) drew penetrating *Egow*'s from them. We had opened a demijohn of red wine, and the aluminum cup went from hand to hand.

When they had all left, Voiné let us in on his new plan: we would propose to the witch-doctors that they organize expiatory ceremonies at Tuwelu, to be restricted to the men; they would agree to that, and we would be able to witness more secret rites.

———

Since dawn the assembly had been debating; our presence had not been required. Hours went by. Finally Voiné ran back, victorious: he had succeeded in persuading them.

"Come on, come on. They'll tell you themselves."

A tall old man with a skin like parchment, wearing a turban and a white tunic, and obviously the spiritual head of the assembly, informed us of the results of the deliberations; his expression was morose. Voiné and Zézé, under orders from the other witch-doctors, were to sacrifice a bull, a cock, and a ram. We would enter the sacred wood to observe the secret rites, but at our own risk and peril: any untattooed men who saw the Great Spirit would die, as well as those who had permitted them access to his domain. Normally all the witch-doctors would attend the expiatory ceremonies;

but because of the danger (real to the Toma) only those whom no fear could paralyze would go.

A rapid glance around the semicircle was enough: we were far from having unanimous support. Sullen faces were numerous. Our avowed enemies were submitting temporarily to a majority decision, but they remained our enemies, and they had become the enemies of Zézé and Voiné now.

"They'll organize a conspiracy against us," Voiné said, worried. "Give me a hundred francs for a red tunic. When they organize a conspiracy against you, you need a red tunic. At night your enemies dream of you in that color, and they can't hurt you." *

Voiné gave us no explanation of the origin of that belief, but he had earned an addition to his wardrobe.

Mamady seemed very satisfied. He had managed to do what we wanted without intervening personally and without abusing his authority in our favor. Before returning to his village, he came to say good-by. The official interpreter was with him, a young man, rather shy, in an elegant white suit and shoes with triple crepe soles. He spoke a highly refined French; his turns of phrase reminded us of Kowo's style.

"I wouldn't mind a little wine," Mamady said genially. The demi-john was still available, in a corner of the hut. Conversation became cordial and lively. Mamady told us about the war in the Rif, and of Casablanca in the time of the conquest. Night fell, and he was still with us; he decided to postpone his departure until morning.

We had already described high points in Western civilization to

* See Appendix, IV: "An Explanation of Dreams."

our guests: circulation of hot and cold water, faucets, means of transportation—particularly the airplane with no motor, the jet plane—and of course the subway, elevators, restaurants. . . .

In turn, we tried to get them to tell us about the great forest and its animals. In lively phrases they described their panther- and antelope-hunts. Voiné listened with a condescending expression. He despised the interpreter, who was his rival with one of Mamady's daughters.

"And the elephants," I prompted Mamady. I had noticed immense signal-horns that played the same part in villages that drums did in cities; they were hollowed out of ivory tusks.

"I've never seen an elephant," Mamady admitted. "Nobody here has ever seen one. They're over on the other side of Beyla."

I told them, and watched their amazement grow, that the white men had succeeded in taming elephants, and was soon explaining what a circus was; the lion-tamer with his head in the big cat's mouth filled them with admiration.

"But the white man fears nothing," Mamady said. "I have even heard that they hold truck races."

"Also bicycle races," Voiné said, wanting the last word. "When I was with the white fathers at the mission, I won the big race."

In the afternoon of the next day, under a leaden sky, we left for Tuwelu. Voiné was wearing his new protective tunic: an ox-blood Lacoste shirt that he had noticed the day before at a Diula's stall.

Storms broke around us all day. They would be more frequent

during the following weeks. The rainy season was almost upon us.

At night, barefoot, hunched against the torrential rain, we approached Tuwelu. The swift, shallow streams had doubled in volume. We slid on the wet clay of the trail. Tall shrubs scratched at our faces. We stumbled over enormous windfall branches. The blackness was complete. Only the lightning, slashing constantly across the dark sky, guided us.

Now and then I caught a glimpse of Voiné, ahead, his dripping black hat jammed down over his ears. "Watch out," he said, turning once in midstream, "watch out, it's *swarming!*"

Soaked through, exhausted, we trudged into the village. Voiné looked like a lamppost sprayed with red lead; his tunic had run all over him. He had seen us every day taking notes; now he declared, suddenly: "White men who hike through the bush like animals, I never saw that before. You suffer too much. I'll have to write about your sufferings."

"But you don't know how to write," Virel said.

"You can write it for me. I'll tell you what to put down."

Since early morning black clouds had been hovering over the forest. Would we have enough light to shoot the film? Today the high expiatory ritual was to take place. For a week now Voiné and Zézé had become more and more worried; they had covered the region in all directions, trying to undo, link by link, the growing conspiracy (it surrounded us now like a net) and consulting the more famous witch-doctors. Among the Toma, the witch-doctor and the soothsayer share the world of magic between them. The witch-doctor, guardian and repository of tribal secrets, knows the rites and sacrifices, battles the evil spirits, transmits the Afwi's will, and can, if he is also a wizard, cast spells; but it is incumbent on the soothsayer to unveil the future and to fix the nature and date of the sacrifices. Between soothsayers and witch-doctors, whose functions overlap constantly, there are frequent rivalries.

But the problem was so serious that Zézé had not hesitated to go even to his enemies for aid. Also, there might have been a political reason behind his overtures.

One last time Zézé questioned the village soothsayer, his best friend, old Wego. Seated around Wego in the semidarkness of the hut, we waited anxiously for the prophecy. Wego, squatting on a mat, shook out a handful of many-colored stones, beans, and hard polished kernels from a little skin bag. He threw them out before him, gathered in several of them with a quick motion, and laid out a mysterious geometric pattern. He plunged his hand into the bag again, and little by little traced what was virtually a written page on the ground. Then, his head in his hands, he drew himself tightly together; we were all staring at him. He raised an impassive face toward us, and spoke so slowly that his lips barely moved. Voiné, absorbed, forgot to interpret.

"Wait," he said. "Later."

The soothsayer's conclusions were brief. The ceremony must take place today, even if the other witch-doctors did not come; and tonight we would pass the second obstacle and enter the sanctum sanctorum, restricted to the elite among the initiated, where we would sacrifice a dog on the great mask, the incarnation of the Afwi.

Consultation fee: one red rooster, its neck to be slit over the ancestral tomb.

Until the very last moment Zézé, sitting dejectedly in front of his hut, waited for the principal witch-doctors invited. The afternoon wore on. It was useless to delay any longer. All those who would come were there, personal friends of Zézé; a few inquisitive people from the neighboring village had joined them. One of them, in an old khaki uniform, came up to us, and said: "I'm Private Noel Akoi. Just back from the war in Indochina. But I left here before I was tattooed, and now the others don't let me into all their ceremonies. If I come with you they won't say anything."

We saw no reason to deny him that satisfaction; the inhabitants of Tuwelu obviously did not consider him one of their own, but showed no animosity toward him. According to the witch-doctors, only six Toma out of approximately fifteen thousand were not tattooed. Noel Akoi's position was difficult. After taking courses at the mission school, he had gone on with his studies in Conakry, and then joined the army. Wounded and sent home, he had been discharged two years before; but, a convert to Catholicism, he had refused to submit to the tribal laws, and lived as a foreigner in his own country.

"I saw buffaloes work in Indochina," he told us, "and I wanted to do the same thing here; I could have worked a much larger farm. But the whole country rose up against me, and my own father forbade me to do it. 'If you can be that cruel to animals, we don't want you here. Go back with the white men.' So I had to give it up."

The dark vault of clouds yielded; a ray of sunlight brightened the village. Zézé settled into his carved chair, surrounded by all the elders, by all the men. He waited in the center of the square. Two young boys set at his feet the sacrificial knife and the ritual objects: bundles of *guinzé*, kola nuts, a flat black basket, and the long, straight saber, emblem of what had once been the warrior caste. An old man with a white beard, the blind man of Tuwelu, rose and delivered a panegyric to the ancestors. Then, his arms spread wide, he invoked the spirits of the forest. He recited his incantations in a monotone. With one voice, the crowd responded: *"Egow!"* to every phrase, their palms raised to the sky. The animals were led forth: a superb young bull, a black and white ram with spiraling horns, and a red cock. The sun disappeared again.

I had already seen many animals slaughtered in Toma country, where sacrifice is an everyday affair, but this time a painful sensation had hold of me. That kind of ceremony had never before seemed cruel, stark. The officiating butcher, with one long, expert, precise stroke of his knife for each, cut the beasts' throats and then left them. The bull, hobbled, his head attached to his withers only by the spinal column, tried to rise out of pools of blood; the ram struggled to his feet, staggered, and collapsed, his legs stiff, with a last quiver. The decapitated cock hopped crazily on the stones, jerked wildly, and fell between two rocks. The men, gloomy, hardly dared watch. The omens contradicted one another. The silent crowd scattered slowly under a great sky, sad as a sky of winter.

An oblique ray of sunlight shot out between two clouds. A play of hard shadow and lively light flickered over the village. The door of the medicine hut, the Toma temple, opened. Zézé and Wego came out, pitchforks in hand, wearing all their talismans. Behind them a man bore on his shoulder a large wooden statue of a woman, crowned with the crest of a helmet, and wearing a grayish tunic; her arms circled by copper rings, she was hung with necklaces of glass beads.

We felt a storm imminent, but Voiné seemed unworried. "When Vollolibei comes out, it can't rain."

Vollolibei, the name of the statue, means, according to Voiné: "So beautiful is it that you stand watching until the sun has set." Probably the translation is a little free. Tuwelu's Vollolibei was female; the male lived in a neighboring village. Sometimes a great ceremony was organized to bring them together, and the two danced to the voice of the Afwi. Today Vollolibei would be alone, because the invited witch-doctors had not answered Zézé's call; but the will of the spirits would be done in spite of all bad omens, and the procession began.

In a trance, indifferent to everything, his face raised to the threatening sky, Zézé sang in a voice we would not have called his. Behind him a witch-doctor bore the statue. Then came the men, singing in chorus. The storm swept down on the village like a tidal wave. The forest trembled. Leaves ripped from treetops spun in whirlwinds of burning air. Zézé defied all the evil forces: he repelled them with his trident. His voice took on a formidable volume. Roused by battle against the loosed elements, the men answered, bellowing.

Voiné, beside us, was shaking with truly hysterical laughter. "It never rains when Vollolibei comes out," he repeated. "Zézé is stronger than all of them. He'll chase the storm away."

The dénouement seemed inevitable. Already great gusts of rain had drowned the near-by hills; flashes of lightning multiplied, streaking across the black sky. Men's voices were lost in the constant rumble of thunder. They set Vollolibei on the ground. Alone, stronger than Zézé, she would fight the storm.

Too late: the first waves of rain, thick, opaque, attacked the village. Zézé seemed not disappointed but furious. Carried by Voiné, Vollolibei hurried back to the obscurity of the medicine hut, and for the first time we entered it ourselves.

From the ceiling laths, varnished by smoke, long cobwebs hung, heavy with dust, like funeral veils. Back in the depths of a niche full of talismans lay the old chest containing a pottery mask of the Afwi; to each side rose wicker baskets, their sides covered with dogs' skulls. Zézé, Wego, and Voiné, squatting around Vollolibei in the center of the hut, were tossing kola nuts; they fell well. The storm, in full blast now, was therefore not the work of the forest spirits. Zézé raised Vollolibei's tunic, revealing her pubic region; Voiné blew ground kola meat over it. This rite would appease her wrath for good. Our friends were a little more cheerful; the master witch-doctor stared at us, and said, through Voiné:

"The spirits are with us. Only the evil witch-doctors have launched bush-devils against me, but I am not afraid. Tonight I lead you to the place where only the initiates may go. You will see the Great Spirit, and I will sacrifice my dog to him."

That night, after the storm, the forest seemed denser and noisier than usual, seemed to hang thickly over the village. Footsteps approached our hut. Voiné entered and very carefully set an old bottle of rum near the lantern.

"Stand up," he said in a dry tone. "I'll have to wash your faces."

We had known of this rite. No one was permitted to appear before the Great Spirit without having laved his face in magic water. Voiné poured a few drops into the hollow of his hand, and we were anointed one by one. The fresh, sweetish odor of the liquid recalled that of the wet woods.

"Now come."

We had already prepared our photographic equipment: magnesium flares, cameras, the generator. We followed our guide into the black night.

At the far end of the clearing in which we had once heard the Afwi's immense voice, a narrow path opened. Voiné raised his lantern, cut two very straight green branches, set them at the head of the trail in the form of a cross, and started forward: by that one operation he had erected a magical barrier that no Toma would dare overstep. Beyond the cross and down the path, the witch-doctors were waiting in a pocket of forest hardly even cleared. By the gleam of the lantern I saw among them, on the ground, a black mask almost a yard high, half crocodile, half ram, slimy with the blood of sacrifices, stuccoed with ground kola meat. Zézé, squatting, was comforting his dog with tender gestures. Fichter groped nervously in the camera-case.

"We've forgotten the film for reloading," he said in a low voice.

The ceremony was beginning; nothing could hold it off; and neither Fichter, the cameraman, nor Tony, the photographer, nor I could chase after the film.

Virel made the decision, grabbed a lantern, and ran back up the trail. The village was hard by; in five minutes at most he'd be back. Meanwhile we could shoot the first reel.

Zézé was worried, uneasy. He was sorry to have let us pass the second barrier, but there was no turning back now. He threw out the kola nuts, still caressing his dog, and began his incantations in a barely audible voice. Suddenly a confused shout ripped through the night. It was Virel. The natives were on their feet, furious. No voice could violate the silence of the sacred wood. Voiné, who considered us under his tutelage, tried vainly to guide Virel, imitating animal cries. Virel, probably in a bad way, couldn't distinguish them from other forest noises and went on calling. Zézé and Voiné plunged into the bush to find him. The other witch-doctors eyed us bitterly.

A few minutes later Zézé was back in the clearing, followed by Voiné and Virel, the latter bewildered and empty-handed. It was not the time for explanations. The witch-doctors, in a hurry now, began the ceremony immediately. Zézé took up his incantations, and tested the edge of his knife on a blade of grass. Then, brutally, hands came out of the shadows and seized the dog, muzzling him to cut off his whimpering. A solemn sacrifice was being consummated. All the witch-doctors bore grave expressions. Their emotion gave me a glimpse of what human sacrifice might mean among the Toma.*

The animal had not even resisted; his blood showered over the

* See Appendix, V: "Press Clipping."

THE SACRED FOREST

mask, and the witch-doctors laid him gently on the ground, covering his head with a wide leaf.

Wego stripped. Naked from top to toe, he stooped and slipped under the panther- and monkey-skins of the heavy black mask. The skins fell to his knees when he rose; he held the mask at temple-height, and the incarnation of the Great Spirit had come to life before our eyes. It whirled slowly before Vollolibei, whom Voiné held out at arm's length. Lantern-flame glittered darkly off the blood-soaked mask, off the drops falling to the skins.

The ceremony ended in silence, and we broke up to go back to the village in groups, by different paths.

For quite a while, lying in our hammocks, we found nothing to say. We held Virel's blunder against him; it might have cost us the trust of the witch-doctors—and he knew it. He decided to break the painful silence.

"Tomorrow I'll find Zézé. I'll explain what happened in the woods."

When we awoke in the morning he was already gone. We learned that he was in Zézé's hut; they had been parleying since daybreak.

We were downing our morning tea when he came back. Zézé, behind him, seemed quite satisfied. We held back our questions in the witch-doctor's presence, but as soon as we were alone, we jumped on Virel.

"All I did was tell him about my dream last night," Virel said. He described it to us. He was alone in the sacred wood, lost among the thorns and lianas, feeling suffocated, when the dog rose up before him and made him understand that he was to follow. Suddenly, deep night became day; the rooster crowed, and he found himself in the clearing, at dawn, watching the sacrifice of the dog.

Zézé told him that the Afwi had surely spoken to him through this dream; that the Afwi had confused him deliberately the night before, to manifest his powers and to delay the sacrifice of the dog, which should not, in principle, have taken place before dawn.

"Then he gave me his blessing," Virel finished, "and said to me: 'If you had black skin, you'd be my equal as a witch-doctor.' Then I gave him money for the sacrifice of a red rooster in my name."

———

Virel's explanations had raised his prestige, and by extension our own; Zézé had now forgotten his momentary anger. Every day he spent long hours in our hut, talking about Toma customs. He never hesitated to furnish whatever information we wanted, but occasionally he failed to grasp the meaning of a question.

The sacrifice of the dog in the sacred wood had made a sharp impression on all of us, and the image of the great black mask, with a crocodile's snout and a ram's horns, was burned into our memories. "What do you call that mask?" I asked Zézé.

"Okobuzogui, the Afwi's nephew."

Little by little I dragged out of him all that we wanted to know on the topic. Okobuzogui took his name from one of Zézé's ancestors, the founder of the village, the one whose footprint remained in the great black boulder. Okobuzogui was the secret incarnation of the great forest spirit. Women and non-initiates were forbidden to behold him, under pain of death; so he was brought forth only at night. Sometimes, during exceptionally important ceremonies, he came abroad in full daylight and toured the village. The women were then required to flee far into the bush.

"Is he the most important of all the fetishes?"

"No. The Afwi himself—no one ever sees him—is the strongest of all. He is the union of all the Toma people."

Now we understood the other witch-doctors' rage. Zézé had revealed to us not a personal secret, as Voiné had in showing us Angbai, but the great tribal secret. All other fetishes were of lesser importance; certain of them even had their origins among neighboring tribes; but the magic powers they conferred upon their cult could be bought with sacrifices and offerings, or even as a simple piece of merchandise. The Vollolibei, for example, came from the Sierra Leone; and among all the forest personalities we had met, only three were properly of Toma origin: Angbai, "the man bearing hides"; Laniboi, "the dancer on stilts"; and Wenilegagui, "the bird-man." The first two had to speak Toma, under penalty of a fine; Wenilegagui was mute. As for the Bakorogui, a bearded mask, guardian of the sacred wood, he had been borrowed from the Guerzé, a neighboring tribe whose customs were very similar to those of the Toma, and who spoke only Toma. Another category of bird-men, the Zavelegui, whose faces too were hidden by feathers, had purchased their secrets from the Malinké.

"And," Voiné added, "it's very strong medicine."

———

I was a little bewildered by the constant confusion of mask and medicine. I had no idea what meaning Voiné gave to the latter word, but by being very patient I finally won an explanation. When Voiné sacrificed the termite queen, he had set talismans and a miniature of the great mask on Angbai. These objects gave the fetish all its value. Without them it would have no magic power; on the other hand the talismans, even alone, retained all their efficacy. Zézé explained the composition of the medicines. On the whole it was fairly similar to the more extravagant recipes of traditional white man's witchcraft, maybe a touch more exotic: to fingernail parings and human hairs were occasionally added a termite queen, or strips of human flesh shredded from corpses or gathered up after the initiation rites. Medicines differed widely, according to the desired end: one of the most rare and most effective was called, according to our witch-doctors, "the gri-gri that breathes." Its preparation involved a number of sacrifices, and a condition difficult to fulfill: it had to be wrapped in a red flannel belt stolen from an infantryman of the French Army.

"If you have that," Voiné finished, "all your enemies fear you. When you look at it, you see it move. To take it from one place to another, you have to hold it in your arms, up tight against you, and run without breathing. When you're out of breath, you have to set it down and begin again a little later."

Then he told us a story; its authenticity was, to him, indisputable.

In the time of force, the French commander ordered the witch-doctors to come to Macenta and turn in all their medicines. They obeyed, in fear of punishment. But on the way, before reaching the city, they stopped for one last magical ceremony. The strongest of all invoked the forest spirits; at his call, bush-devils surged forth and raised a wind so terrible that it snatched away all the roofs and destroyed many huts in Macenta. The commander sent a soldier to tell them to take everything back to their villages; he had no wish to keep such dangerous medicine at the post.

"And that is all written in the books," Voiné said, "at the office, in Macenta."

The night of the ceremony I had not been able to single out Okobuzogui, and now Zézé offered to show it to us. After the sacrifice he had left it in the sacred wood. "Now you have the right to enter," he said. "But the women had better not see you."

Voiné led us along a winding trail, and soon we caught up with the master witch-doctor in the little clearing; he was squatting in front of the mask. On a bed of banana leaves lay Okobuzogui, in the midst of spread hides. He seemed less terrifying by day than he had the night of the sacrifice, sweating fresh blood in the harsh light of a magnesium flare. Zézé pointed out a very small piece of black earthenware. "That's the medicine that makes Okobuzogui powerful."

Then he stripped again, donned the mask, and told Voiné that we could photograph him. He could have given us no greater proof of his trust and friendship than by thus defying custom.

When we were back in the village, Voiné stopped in front of a large hut. "Here is the women's medicine. Look at it without touching it and without asking questions; you'll see it, right opposite the doorway."

Within, three fat old women were bustling around. Two of them were spinning cotton. One, her hair wild and stiff, her eyes circled with white lime, must have been in mourning for a relative. The third, squatting beside a cook-pot, kept an eye on rice boiling over a wood fire. Three stones laid out in the center of the hut were the hearth.

They rose to greet us and seemed very happy that we had dropped in. Through Voiné, we exchanged the usual courteous phrases. They invited us to sit down and offered us a handful of kola nuts. We examined the hut leisurely: it was a large whitewashed room, with a wide bench running around the four walls; the room was divided into alcoves, each reserved for one of the women and her children. The ceiling was as sooty and as dusty as that of the men's medicine hut. In a niche opposite the doorway I noticed a sort of miniature hut, like a doll-house, next to which stood a small termite column, emptied of its inhabitants and crowned with an earthenware pot. Above it, talismans were hung at different levels on the wall, each rolled in a small mat. The women's medicine was doubtless in the miniature hut.

Madame Chef set to work cleaning some whitish vegetables. They were long-stemmed bush mushrooms. "Tonight you'll eat mushrooms à la Toma," Voiné said. "I'll ask the old lady, and you can make her a little present."

We questioned one another silently, but the desire to vary our menu won out.

Voiné decided that our visit had lasted long enough and gave the signal to leave. The three old women followed us out to the middle of the square and covered us with benedictions, repeating: *"Balika, balika."*

"*Balika*" means "thank you" in Malinké. Malinké was the only foreign language the Toma knew. As we were foreigners ourselves, they naturally used it with us, in the hope of being better understood.

"That was the first time white men have been in their hut," Voiné said. "They thought you were very gallant."

The chicken and mushrooms (prepared by Voiné, who occasionally condescended to take over the cuisine) were succulent. No sign of bellyache in the morning; no ptomaine poisoning.

Voiné was quite pleased.

During the day we went on with our interrogation of Zézé on the origin of the masks, but this time I sensed that he wasn't following the questions.

"At the very beginning of the world," I asked him, "the bush spirits existed, didn't they?"

Bewildered, Zézé stared at me; I must have seemed very stupid.

"But no," he said, shrugging. "Us, the Zogui, we do all that."

He explained the word; I hadn't heard it before. "Zogui" meant literally "man," but he was using it in this more limited sense: "the great witch-doctor, the master of the forest spirits, the whole man."

"When the earth was born," he added, "all that existed was water, the serpent, and two medicines: the Belimassai and the Zazi."

These two words referred to the same thing: the "thunderstone." But the first was used by men, and the second by women.

While we were on genesis, I made another stab at the Toma legends of the creation of the world and the first man; and as usual I came up against not reluctance but total ignorance. For the witch-doctors, the most ancient memories were of the generation before the arrival of the white man. Naturally, as a product of Western civilization I was unable to conceive of men who had never wondered about their own origin. Perhaps the disorder following the irruption of French troops into the country was sufficient to cut off transmission of oral traditions and to replace them by war legends, which were recited to us in every village we ran across.

Now it was night, and the witch-doctors had left us. Sitting on a crate near the lantern, I was rereading my notes and trying to make sense out of what Zézé and Voiné had told us.

The medicine tunic, object of Voiné's ambitions, belonged to Zézé, and Zézé alone possessed its magic powers. The different masks and talismans belonged to a certain category of witch-doctors. The female Vollolibei of Tuwelu protected the village, but was incomplete without the male of a near-by settlement. Okobuzogui himself was powerless beyond the district limits. The effectiveness of these medicines, to use Voiné's word, lay (aside from their claimed magical powers) in operations intended to provoke fear (the imitation of beasts bellowing; fierce disguises) or to create an atmosphere favorable to manifestations of the supernatural.

But the Afwi, invisible and omnipotent, grouped all the Toma. Their magic was essentially a collective phenomenon. "The spirit of three men is stronger than one man," Voiné had told me.

In as involute a community as a native village, if a dozen men hold a meeting in the sacred wood to sentence a tribesman to punishment or death, the latter has obviously no chance to escape his fate. Without recourse to force, by simple suggestion, the witch-doctors can oblige their victim to do their will. When necessary, if the victim rebels, they can help him to die. All witch-doctors handle poison with great skill, and Voiné, during our hikes through the bush, had shown us lianas, fruits, or barks from which they could be extracted. This knowledge is part of the witch-doctor's armory.

I began to understand why old Zézé, great Zogui though he was, could be uneasy about the conspiracy being brewed by his enemies. Before reaching the level of detachment he displayed now toward the ancestral beliefs, he had shared those beliefs. He was himself bound by the secret he imposed on others: his quality as master witch-doctor permitted him to use the collective magic forces at will; but he could neither flee from nor betray that universe of which he was part, without fearing retribution in kind. His alliance with us had placed him in a serious position: by divulging their secrets he had lost the support of the great mass of the Toma, who were re-grouping around his enemies, who in turn had him at their mercy. He could not deny the forces he himself had controlled for so long, and he was afraid of them.

But Toma magic could not be summed up so easily. We had not succeeded in solving the riddle of our first night in the country, of the lightning in Doezia, of the two (or three) Voinés in Sagpaou. And then, when Zézé said: "It is the men who have made every-thing," he was not giving us his personal point of view on the forest spirits, but the general feeling of all the witch-doctors; and when he repelled the storm with his pitchfork, repeating magic formulas handed down by his predecessors, he believed in their effectiveness; if the incantations failed, then to save the situation he called upon his intelligence.

CHAPTER SIX

115

I argued with myself among all these contradictions, realizing that they did not seem so to the Toma and bothered them not at all. All the reactions that I attributed to Zézé, all the explanations I devised of his attitude, were valid only for me, the white man. Zézé himself was concerned with fewer problems, and in any case formulated them in an entirely different manner.

At that very moment, in his hut, he must have been trembling with fear, the insurmountable fear of punishment by the spirits, spirits created by men, but whose power he would not dream of challenging. Women and children were afraid of the Bakorogui, and yet knew that under the terrifying mask a flesh-and-blood man was hidden; the initiates recoiled before Okobuzogui; and Voiné himself was afraid of Zézé in the medicine tunic, and dreamed of owning one. His reactions ran counter to our European taste and logic. The attitudes might seem childish to us, but they had to be allowed if we were to understand the Toma. We were seeking to resolve contradictions; they were simply living them.

———

During the previous few days the conspiracy had taken on a growing importance in Voiné's conversation and thought. After a short period of truce the witch-doctors of the region had set their malediction on us again.

Voiné could no longer arrive at our hut in the morning without announcing either: "The conspiracy is upon us," or "The conspiracy is broken," depending on the result of his nosing around in near-by villages. We began to bet among ourselves on each morning's announcement.

Today, though, we all lost our bets.

"I have an idea," Voiné said as he came in, followed by Zézé. "We ought to go see Darazu, the great charlatan."

For him that word, which he pronounced with respect, implied one of the highest degrees of magical power.

The soothsayer Darazu Koiwogui, of the village of Anorezia, was almost Zézé's equal, and was directing the cabal against us in the name of ancestral laws. Voiné and Zézé, after ripe reflection, had decided that it would be politic on our part to see him face to face.

We had left Tuwelu very early in the morning, and had already passed through several small villages.

"Stop," Voiné ordered abruptly. "Darazu carries the gri-gri that breathes. I'll have to wash your faces with magic water or you'll be helpless."

We submitted to that rite, and shortly afterward reached Anorezia. Half the village lay in neglected ruins. High grass had covered the rocky soil around collapsed huts with shattered roofs. As always around noon, the inhabitants were working their patches of land, and the village seemed abandoned. Finally we managed to find an elder, who pointed out the soothsayer's hut.

Darazu was an obese colossus with tiny shrewd eyes. Three braids of hair lay on his shaved head, in the old-fashioned Toma manner; they and his moon-face made him seem more Asiatic than Negro. From the first word, he refused to speak to us outside the presence of the village chief, and sent for a runner, who went off to the chief's *lugan*. While we waited, the great charlatan led us into an empty hut and settled himself across from us. Two of his wives brought us gourds of fresh water.

Voiné rolled frightened eyes and made a sign that we should accept nothing. But all four of us drank, to demonstrate our faith in Darazu. Then we sat for a good while, motionless, across from the silent soothsayer.

Finally the village chief arrived, escorted by all the elders, who grouped around us.

Voiné transmitted my request: "I wish to speak with Darazu alone, or, if he insists, in the chief's presence."

They seemed very reticent. Among the Toma, differences are generally settled by force, and here we were the enemy. We invited them to notice that we had no arms, and that they ran no risk.

After long hesitation, Darazu made up his mind and guided us to a small clearing outside the village. I attacked with all the arguments that had won over others. Seated beside me, so as not to have to look at me, his eyes half-shut, his head bowed, he traced tiny patterns in the sand with a twig. I saw immediately that he would never be our ally. In his eyes, we had committed an irreparable fault, meriting exemplary punishment. Over and above that, Darazu was interested in Zézé's job.

"I don't ask you to help us," I finished; "only to do nothing against us."

He did not answer right away. A sarcastic smile appeared on his lips. Across from him Jean, tense, contained himself with great difficulty.

Finally Darazu raised his head and defined his point of view. He assured us of his warmest personal feelings and informed us that if the village chief had authorized it, he would certainly have appeared at the ceremonies in Tuwelu. Unfortunately, no one had notified him. (We all knew he was lying. We had seen him in Doezia.) He went on, intimating that he had no objection at all to our knowing the secrets of the sacred wood, but that he would have no part in revealing them to us himself.

"I am too afraid of death."

His duplicity was obvious. We got nothing out of him. It was useless to insist. Beside him the village chief, eyes blank, lower lip pendant, face servile, punctuated Darazu's declarations with expressionless *Egow*'s. He had no idea what was going on—that was evident—and his whole role consisted in approving Darazu's decisions automatically.

"I won't do anything to obstruct you," the great charlatan repeated one last time. He wanted only one thing: to see us leave. The interview was a failure. After the formulas required by courtesy, we left him.

On the way back I caught up to Voiné, ahead of us on the trail. He was morose; I told him how disappointed I was.

"The people in Anorezia are too smart," he said sententiously. "They elected the biggest idiot of all as chief. That way, when the district chief gives them an order they don't like, they don't do a thing, and afterward they say that the village chief doesn't know how to command. But if you try to get them to change the village chief, nothing doing. They won't even hear of it."

CHAPTER SIX

Thursdays we took turns (the trip was no fun at all) riding into Macenta to pick up mail, on the truck of a native merchant who came to the Tuwelu market for supplies. This week it was my turn, but Jean wanted to come with me. According to the last letters we had had from Paris, two weeks before, the birth of his boy was imminent. Of course, it could only be a boy. Jean was taking huge strides toward the post office, dragging me behind him, almost before the truck had stopped in the market place.

The mail had come in the day before, and the sorting wasn't finished. Jean, in his impatience, delivered a sharp critique of the postal administration both in France and in Africa, and then of the local employees' nonchalance. Even so, the clerks put up full steam to please him, slinging mailbags wildly, scrabbling among packets of printed matter. Finally, beaming, they handed him a telegram a week old. Jean, livid, opened it feverishly, jammed it into a pocket, and left without a word, to the clerks' great disappointment. I thanked them for him and caught up with him.

He was glaring straight ahead. "It's a girl," he said. "And as if that wasn't enough, they've called her Virginia!"

By "they" I could see that he meant all humanity; he held the world responsible for the birth of his daughter and for a romantic name he thought ridiculous. I pointed out that I had survived a similar tragedy during the Orinoco-Amazon expedition, and assured him that men learned to live with anything.

Our few European friends in Macenta tried to console him with apéritifs. Wasted effort; on this point his reactions were those of a pure Toma. On the other hand the apéritifs made us miss the return truck. After dinner our friends invited us to an open-air movie, the town's latest innovation.

Out beyond the native village, between two awnings supported by poles, a little sixteen-millimeter projector threw rather vague images on a more or less stretched sheet. The humming of the generator often drowned out the actors' voices and the tremulous music. On the rutted ground, crude benches, overloaded with spectators, swayed dangerously.

A majority of the public was African. With passionate interest they followed wars among bacilli and microbes, encouraging the adversaries loudly, during a documentary on the work of Pasteur. A short about wrestling hardly raised as much enthusiasm. There followed, without intermission, a good old-fashioned farce; the gags were indecipherable, even for us; but representatives of the master race in long underwear and garters, chased by enormous and indignant matrons, in a slick modern setting, roused storms of wild laughter.

We left before the end and went to order a beer at Foromo's; Foromo was the "number-one *gargotier*" of Macenta. In his large hut, floored with tamped earth, booths had been set up, separated by adobe partitions. On the walls, painted with sham bricks, advertising posters were hung: friendly young ladies vaunted the excellence of various brews. The customers were many and noisy. Several of them were playing *fao*. Others sat quietly, drinking beer or red wine.

Foromo, tall, massive, with a merry face, led us to an empty booth. "Beseat yourselves, gentlemen, beseat yourselves," he insisted, pointing to a rough-hewn bench. After serving us, he introduced us to his vintage customers, in particular Koli Zumanigui, district chief of Baezia.

"That's right," Zumanigui approved, stroking his short mustache. "Seventeen years I've been district chief."

"And never been poisoned?" I asked the question in the tone of voice of a man perfectly acquainted with local customs. A district chief can be the object of much envy.

Zumanigui's tiny, shining eyes squinted. "No. I'm a lot too smart."

He sat down and chatted with us. Koli had heard about all our difficulties, and announced himself as ready to help us. He invited us to an important ceremony for young girls that was supposed to take place in his village a few weeks later.

Then he left us, and we went home with our friends for the night; tomorrow we would find a truck to take us back to Bofosso.

———

Tony and Virel were waiting for us at the base camp, where they had gathered all the film and sound-track so far shot. During the previous two months we had managed (exceeding all hopes) to film the sacred rights of the Toma, and to record the savage music of the Afwi. But an essential problem remained to be solved: how could we guarantee our presence at the initiatory ceremonies in Soguru? The true rainy season was coming on, and the date of that solemn occasion had not even been set.

Also, the hidden opposition of most of the witch-doctors reduced our chances to nil, or practically nil. And yet for Voiné there was never any doubt of our admission to the "great tattooing." Zézé Sohowogui, grand master of the initiation, had presided over that ceremony seven times. With his support, anything was possible.

To confound our enemies, Voiné had decided to call upon the forest spirits, and this morning he was going to sacrifice a white rooster at the dwelling of his protective genius. We went with him. He struck out directly for the riverbank, where the women were doing laundry. From there we followed a barely visible path quite a way downstream, to the foot of a high cascade, in the deep shadow of the forest. A little way back in the thickest bush, a small fault opened out between two boulders; in the hollow shone a small pond of black water. Voiné knelt before this hole, prostrated himself, and began his prayers to the spirits; then he beheaded the white rooster, which hopped hesitantly for a moment and then dropped into the water, wings outspread.

"The sacrifice has fallen well," Voiné said, rising. "The conspiracy will be broken."

Coming back along the riverbank, he stopped at the foot of a small peninsula where a few trees stood. A narrow platform of tamped earth, surrounded by shrubbery, had been erected there. In its center, on a large black stone, offerings were laid out, rice or pimentoes, in flat black baskets, under the shelter of a cotton awning hung between two branches. These were sacrifices to the serpent.*

---

* See Appendix, VI and VII: "The Sacrifice to the Serpent" and "To be Protected by the Serpent."

"If the serpent accepts your gifts," Voiné said, "if he eats the eggs you bring him, he'll protect you forever. The serpent never lies."

I remembered then that, for the Toma, water and the serpent had existed before man, and, consequently, even before the Afwi.

Our faces haggard, our beards scraggly, we were beginning to show signs of jungle fatigue; we were covered with small squares of adhesive where we had been gnawed by multitudes of insects, abundant now with the approach of the rainy season. These few days at Bofosso were almost a vacation for us. Baré's *gargote*, where red wine and canned goods could be had; the bread brought from Macenta; the relative comfort of the hut, with its furniture of crates; the stream where we went to bathe—all this was a change from the rude life of the bush.

Voiné, who spent most of his time doing nothing, convinced us that an assistant was indispensable anyway, and hired a boy of about twelve, little Zézé, who knew three or four words of French, and who was supposed to be very helpful.

His presence served chiefly to raise Voiné's prestige in the eyes of the villagers. Zézé, a skinny boy with a triangular face, was alert, fast on his feet; but he did not have a servant's vocation. He waited on table two or three times, rushing through the meal under Voiné's disapproving eye, and slipping away immediately afterward to go and play with his little friends in the village.

Voiné wanted to take him to Tuwelu, but we had noticed very quickly that he lost his rudimentary vocabulary whenever we asked him to do something, and that he was never around when Voiné needed him. I mentioned this to Voiné.

"That's right," he approved. Then, after reflection, he added: "The boy never does a thing. Somebody ought to kill a cock on his gri-gri; otherwise he'll go crazy."

I had no desire to discuss that last point, and advised him to remit little Zézé to his parents, who could take the necessary measures themselves.

After that brief spell of relaxation we were happy to get back to our hut in Tuwelu. While we were gone, Zézé, who was showing a good deal more anxiety than our witch-doctor guide, had gone on canvassing the region, trying to frustrate Darazu's emissaries.

Their stubbornness amazed me.

"They think you're trying to split the Toma," Voiné told me.

Now and then we made the rounds with Zézé. According to him, we could give the lie to our enemies very effectively by our amicable attitude.

The trails of Gueriguerika became more and more familiar to us, and we could count many friends now in the villages. The Toma seemed much too busy with their farming to worry about us; each year, after the harvest, the *lugans* were abandoned, and the elders decided on the new areas of forest to be cleared. The felled trees were burned on the spot. During this season only the very aged and the infants remained in the villages. Anyone old enough to work cleared brush, dug out tangled roots, and prepared the land for seeding. This arduous task had to be completed before the heavy rains. But when they came home evenings they all dropped by to greet us cordially; their hospitality never flagged. Nothing seemed to justify Zézé's anxiety.

All these wanderings in the forest had confirmed our impression of the great importance attached by the Toma to sacrifices. In every village we ran across ritual objects that we had not previously noticed. Horizontal crosses had been erected on tombs: two billets, holes bored through the middle, slipped over a stem, standing like weathervanes. Stakes almost hidden within a pile of rude quoits, stood in public squares. Wreaths of spiral liana were hung in the huts. Under the thatched awnings, chains of linked liana swayed. All these talismans protected the village or the family against fire, death, disease.

And deep in the bush, far from the villages, narrow paths led occasionally off the trail—led to each man's hidden altar, where he sacrificed to the waters and the serpent.

While Zézé and Voiné sounded out the more celebrated soothsayers, in search of a line of conduct, long days of waiting passed in Tuwelu. The forced inaction became intolerable. We broke it by organizing a layman's infirmary, where we treated cuts, venereal disease, wounds due to the explosion of locally manufactured muskets, and always abscesses; we were almost pleased to see our steady customers each evening.

In the beginning the villagers had not trusted themselves readily to our care, but then we brought about a few sensational cures. Antibiotics like penicillin and aureomycin work like lightning on organisms not already saturated with them; and our patients, mostly women, were more numerous every day at Jean Fichter's clinic. (His skill at injections had promoted him to the rank of expedition doctor.)

One night they brought us an emergency case: a man strangely twisted, covered with cuts, his face and shoulder ripped open by deep gashes. A rapid examination brought out the facts: his huddled posture was congenital; but our patient had fallen from the top of a palm tree. Once the lacerations had been disinfected and filled with sulfanilamide, we closed them up as well as we could with tight ribbons of adhesive; we had no clamps. The injured man started coming out of his shock; after a glass of rum he was in condition to talk.

"That's the third time he's fallen from a palm," Voiné translated.

We advised the patient to give up that form of exercise; he seemed unfitted for it. His left eye, the one that had not disappeared under bandages, expressed profound sorrow.

"He can't quit. That's his job: he's a coconut-picker."

The elders and witch-doctors were in the habit of assembling in our hut. Even in Voiné's absence, we could hold long conversations with them: the patriarch Voiné Beawogui interpreted. His white beard and white hair, his height, his slenderness, the nobility of his gestures, all gave him something of the bearing of the Peuhls, in the Futa-Jallon region. As a child, just after the tattooing, he had left his village to go to work for the whites. Become the *homme de confiance* of a high official, he had accompanied him everywhere, and now spoke almost all the languages of Guinea. He had retired to Tuwelu. Here everyone respected and admired his knowledge, though he refused to practice fetish rituals. He was the village atheist. He absented himself from all ceremonies, and, happier than the veteran Noel Akoi, managed to live at peace with everyone. He was satisfied to concentrate on raising grandchildren of his own persuasion (he was always surrounded by a flock of them) and on tending his farm. Our equipment amazed him, particularly the tape recorder; he badgered us with questions about it, but on the other hand failed to see why we were interested in the sacred wood, or why the witch-doctors were roused against us.

"The white men have planes. They fly high, and they see everything that happens, and they know all the secrets already. They don't hide their secrets from us; why should we hide ours from them?"

Unfortunately, not all the Toma shared this opinion. One evening Zézé returned from a trip utterly dejected. Darazu had succeeded in persuading almost everyone of the gravity of our sacrilege. He maintained that we had filmed secrets for the sole purpose of betraying them to the women and to neighboring tribes, and that we would not keep any of our promises. He had a double object: to bar us from the mass tattooing at Soguru, and to depose Zézé. Expiatory sacrifices and ritual fines had not appeased our enemies' wrath; and I remembered again Prosper Zumanigui's warning in Macenta about the Soguru ceremonies: "To see them, you'll have to be tattooed yourselves."

We had already considered undergoing the initiatory rites. Tonight, after a last unanimous decision, we decided to broach the question directly. We were in agreement; we were even eager to brave the test. It would bring us closer to the Toma and would put an end to an equivocal and more and more painful situation.

When Zézé and Voiné came in, we put it up to them squarely. "You told us that to see the Afwi, a man would have to be tattooed. We would like to be, now."

Voiné was struck dumb. Then he exploded: "Impossible! The old man would never agree!"

He was afraid to translate the request.

Zézé set a hand on his shoulder. Voiné's reaction had not escaped him; he wanted to know.

As Voiné spoke, Zézé's face changed. The two of them stood bemused for a long moment, and left without a word. We waited part of the night for an answer, smoking one cigarette after another. They did not come back.

For a week we attacked, morning and night; when they had returned from the bush; when we met them in the square; when we saw them in our hut. For a week they were caught up in endless parleys with the elders. Their arguments were weighty. No white man had ever been tattooed. Serious risks were involved. Occasionally a Toma failed to survive; what would the other whites say, in Macenta or the towns, if an accident happened? Who could say that the witch-doctors' anger, far from dying, might not redouble? This gesture of obedience to the ritual could either reconcile us with our enemies or be considered the ultimate insult. It was a double-edged weapon.

CHAPTER SEVEN

129

We swore silence, swore to keep the promises already made. We took our risk freely. They ran none, whatever happened.

They went on refusing, stubbornly.

———

"The knife is well sharpened," Voiné said, with an amused smile. "You'll suffer. White skins aren't as tough as black; and even a black man suffers."

That morning, after entering the hut, he had announced brusquely: "You're to be tattooed tonight." And all that day it had been his turn to badger us. With sadistic pleasure he described in detail the different phases of the torment. The witch-doctors had decided. At dawn we would be "eaten by the Great Spirit."

We would follow Voiné and Zézé into the depths of the sacred wood, near the waterfall; its roar would drown our cries. I asked if Zézé would tattoo us himself.

"No," Voiné said. "The old man's quit that now; I do it for him. It's like the district commander in Macenta, the white man's great chief. He never writes himself; the others do it for him."

Wego would come along to hold us in position and to keep us from squirming.

Almost cheerful, we made it a point to joke about the coming test, but our laughs were a little hollow. We prepared the movie equipment carefully, taking a good deal of time. None of us was very eager to meditate on the ceremony, to be alone with his thoughts; we turned in as late as possible.

I dozed off briefly; and a terrifying nightmare jolted me awake. Voiné, gone mad, was slicing through me with swift strokes of his knife, and I couldn't fight back becuase Wego was holding me down with all his strength; my friends, petrified with fear, made no gesture to help me. Awake then, my stomach in knots, I was holding my breath; my telling myself that it was a bad dream, that the tattooing was far from a ritual crime, that there was no real danger, made no difference; my eyes would not close.

Anyway I noticed (with some satisfaction) that none of my companions was really asleep. They tossed and turned and occasionally sighed deeply. I turned to Jean in the hammock next to mine. "You asleep?"

He hitched up on one elbow. "No. No more than you."

And in the darkness we discussed ways and means of shooting the operation. Soon the subject was exhausted, and, silently, each of us returned to his private anguish, finding it intact. . . .

I wondered what time it was. In the village a door creaked on its wooden hinges. Footsteps grated across the gravel in the square and approached our hut. We had all heard; we were standing when Voiné came in, with a rolled mat under his arm.

Without a word we began to dress.

"No," Voiné said, pulling the shirt out of my hand. "Not that."

In shorts, naked to the waist, I was surprised at the night's chill. In shadow, Voiné led us quickly outside the village. At the gateway to the sacred wood he stopped to light his lantern.

"All the earmarks of an old-fashioned execution," Virel murmured.

Wet branches slashed across our faces as we marched. The trip was endless. We stumbled on roots at every step; we bogged down in lianas; we ripped our skins on thorns; but Voiné refused to slow the pace.

"It's three o'clock," Virel said suddenly.

And we understood immediately that Voiné, as much in a hurry as we, had rushed the operation: it was supposed to have been done at dawn.

The roar of the waterfall grew. We emerged into a cleared pocket of forest; Zézé and Wego were waiting for us, sitting near a lantern.

Voiné went back into the woods alone, looking a bit irritated; the other two witch-doctors chatted in low voices. We had no idea how to behave. Virel laid out the first-aid kit, and Jean and I set up the camera and the magnesium flares. Tony had sat down to wait. After a few moments Voiné trotted out of the bush. He had a broken branch in his hand, a branch studded with barbed thorns.

"Turn up the lights," he said.

And he pushed heavily on Virel's shoulders, to bring him to a sitting position; Wego took Virel's arms and straightened them above Virel's head. Wego's motions betrayed a gentleness that could never have been read on his stony face. Virel's body jerked in a spasm of pain. The thorn had penetrated near his right breast. It slipped out. Voiné, impassive, pricked him again, more deeply, raised the skin, and slashed it with a quick stroke of his knife. A drop of blood welled up. Voiné began again a quarter of an inch away.

Now he had been working for ten minutes, and he had finished a kind of half-loop, rising up the middle of Virel's back. Virel had made no sound, but his pale, taut face, his set teeth, his nails digging into Wego's arm, bore witness to his suffering. Several times I thought he would faint; but his will to hold on was stronger.

The third flare died. Voiné stood up. He had just finished the last incision under the right breast, completing the loop. Fifteen minutes had passed since the first. Wego let go of Virel's arm; Virel rose, exhausted, and went to stretch out on the mat Voiné had spread in the shadows.

It was Tony's turn. Selfishly, I drew a relieved breath—a little delay. . . .

This time Voiné was less hesitant. He slashed more surely; the incisions were carefully aligned. His early nervousness was natural. He was the first Toma ever to tattoo a white man. A tiny chain of red droplets grew on Tony's back. Inert, he had let himself relax completely against Wego's thigh; Wego held firmly to his wrists. A little worried, I spoke to Tony: "Okay?"

"Okay," he said in a thin voice. "It's like being cut into strips with a razor. That's the worst."

Finally it was my turn. I saw right away what Tony had meant. I could almost hear the skin split at each stroke. I forced myself to think about other things: a huge luna moth, settling near the lantern; Zézé, opposite me in the shadows, his face solemn, his magic pitchfork in hand; Zézé wearing, God knew why, Voiné's black felt hat; Jean—there was something I wanted to ask Jean about the shooting. I turned my head toward him. He was hunched over the camera. My vision clouded. My ears hummed. A vague nausea stirred in me. I had no idea where Voiné was slicing at that moment.

"Where is he?"

"Just finishing the big loop."

Afterward Jean underwent the torture without incident, or so it seemed—half-conscious, I was paying little attention to him.

We were all stretched out on the mat. A blurred gleam diffused the sky above the treetops. Zézé came out of the shadow and waved his pitchfork over us. Voiné translated:

"You have been eaten by the Great Spirit of the wood. You will forever bear on your bodies the traces of his teeth. Now you are men; Toma, like us."

Virel stood up with great pain and scrabbled in the first-aid kit for a bottle of rum. He passed it around. We swigged long.

"And the witch-doctors?" Voiné asked, sternly.

I gave him the bottle. His hand was trembling a little. He raised the neck to his lips. The rest of us had fallen to the mat again; supine, hands back of our necks, we watched dawn filter through the leaves. Now I could hear again the mingled voices of the forest and the waterfall.

Jean brought out a pack of cigarettes. We followed the spirals of smoke until they were lost in the humid shadows. The taste of tobacco was good.

I wasn't thinking of much. I felt a sort of diffuse happiness. I had been thinking about this step for over a year; it would open an inaccessible domain to us.

My skin shivered lightly.

Jean rose. "I suppose we could go back now," he said. We got

THE SACRED FOREST

up stiffly. We all wanted the hot, humid hut. Moving carefully, pain shooting through our backs, we got our equipment together.

"No you don't," Voiné said. "You stay here. If a woman saw you like that she'd die. I'll get you hammocks and blankets."

And the witch-doctors left us alone, at dawn in the sacred wood.

CHAPTER SEVEN

EIGHT

"Suppose it rained," Tony said. We had no shelter at all, and the scantiest of clothing.

We had awakened fairly late this morning, with aching muscles made torpid by our scarification and by the forest's humidity.

Voiné stood over us, contemplating us with a paternal eye. "It won't rain," he said confidently. "Zézé's Okobuzogui, the big mask of the Afwi, is in the forest near you. As long as he's there, not a drop can fall."

We remembered previous experience, but withheld the obvious comment.

Daubed with Mercurochrome and squatting around the pots of rice Voiné had just brought us, we ate our first true Toma meal. Our witch-doctor deemed silverware dispensable; we dug in with our hands. After the meal Voiné examined our scars with close attention. Our medicines had already proved their effectiveness on many Toma, and the witch-doctors had therefore authorized us to substitute ours for theirs, to shorten our stay in the forest.

Voiné fingered our backs, pressing the scarred tissue in search of infected areas. There was nothing pleasant about the examination, but we were so impatient to leave the forest that we pretended to feel no pain.

"It's going very well. Your medicines are very strong; you'll have to leave me some when you go. In a few days now everything will be dry and you'll be able to get out of the woods."

Voiné was being much more familiar now. To the Toma, there is always a natural bond between the tattooer and the tattooed. He was no longer simply our guide; he was our brother, and he told us, with no reticence, about his own initiation.

"When Zézé did that to me, I screamed much. That's why we brought you out away from the village."

"But you," I said, "you were just a little Bilakoro." He had probably been waiting for that explanation; he just smiled.

Then he told us that Zézé had been tattooed by Wego, which gave us a better idea of their respective ages.

The absence of ritual in our initiation had upset me a little. The witch-doctors had donned no magical ornaments, and no great mask presided at the ceremony; I had no objection to the starkness of the operation, but I was amazed that it should be so.

"You already knew all the secrets," Voiné explained. "You've heard the Afwi. There was nothing left hidden from you. After the initiation we're all men; the masks only come out to scare the women and the Bilakoro."

Besides, he said, we had undergone a ritual initiation, as did those who left the country as children and came back as untattooed adults. When they came back, they were marked with the Great Spirit's seal without ceremony, in the small sacred wood of their village, simply so that they would be able to take their places in the community.

CHAPTER EIGHT

"But is it the same thing at Soguru?" I asked Voiné. Now that we were tattooed, we had a right to know about those ceremonies of collective initiation. If we couldn't catch them on film, at least we wanted to see them.

"No," Voiné said. "The one at Soguru will be a very great ceremony. Not an everyday affair. It takes long preparation."

That was true; the ritual initiation of children took place only once every five to seven years. Several villages assembled, and delimited a vast area of dense forest somewhere in their common territory; trails leading through that area were blocked off and detours set up. An imposing gateway, like the one at Niogbozu, indicated the entrance; its fern roots, handsomely carved, and embellished with ocher, blue, and whitewash, were strangely similar in both matter and style to the ancient statuary of the New Hebrides, on the other side of the world. Access to that gateway would thereafter be restricted to the initiates.

So there were two sacred woods: one of them outside each village, where smaller local ceremonies took place, and the other, much larger, that might be called an "initiation camp," reserved for the tattooing and education of children.

The ceremony itself required several months of preparation. Guelemlai crisscrossed the whole Toma region, announcing to the natives that the day was near, and that they would come soon to take the children away. At the same time they collected offerings, to keep the huge assembly in food and drink; there were often more than three thousand people. Each village had to contribute rice, livestock, palm oil, and a certain amount of money. By their terrifying appearance, the whitened messengers with enormous, flowing horse-collars prepared the climate of fear in which the children would live until their initiation.

On the eve of the great day, runners notified all the villages. Then the witch-doctors loaded baskets with masks and talismans; the men covered themselves with banana leaves until they were entirely hidden; and all left their villages at dusk. From the most remote corners of the Toma region these strange processions converged on the trails to the tattooing ground; lantern-light streaked the night.

The dance began: the tom-tom was absolutely forbidden, and only the multiple voice of the Afwi rose. He was there in his secret incarnations—each village's great black mask participated in the ceremony, and so did the Vollolibei, male and female, united this once. The witch-doctors brought out talismans and charms, and demonstrated, each in his turn, their magical powers.

"Then everybody knows who's strongest," Voiné said. "It's a very dangerous time, because all the poisons are in the air."

At dawn sixty bulls were led into the clearing at the entrance to the sacred wood; all sixty were slaughtered at the same instant. This horrifying butchery took place under the eyes of future initiates and women.

The better cuts of meat were then trimmed away from the victims and stewed with red beans; the stew was presented to the witch-doctors on a wide wooden tray. The witch-doctors poured their most violent poisons onto the tray, most of them based on crocodile bile. The grand master, who would be Zézé Sohowogui, dug out a random morsel with his pitchfork and ate, inviting the others to join him.

"Many witch-doctors die," Voiné commented, laughing. "They don't know all the medicines to use."

That trial confirmed the Zogui's magical powers and his undeniable superiority.*

Long before, the Guelemlai had remitted the children to the bird-men, who were to lead them to the great spirits of the forest; the Wenilegagui cudgeled the children before flinging them over a low wall into the initiation camp. But they followed special rules when dealing with their own sons. The office of Wenilegagui was hereditary; the bird-man chose among his sons the one who would replace him, and before sending him into the sacred wood branded him under the arm with his trident.

On the other side of the wall the witch-doctors received the non-initiates; and there, with no further ceremony, tattooed them immediately, in several groups.

"There are more than two hundred children," Voiné remarked. "That makes many backs to cut."

The children respond to their ordeal in various ways. Some of them scream and fight so madly that they are let off with a few scratches on each side; others, on the contrary, demand more scarring, to prove their courage; but in general no more than three rows of incisions are made on the day of the great initiation. During the time in the bush, the witch-doctors add another each year.

After their ordeal the children must lie on reed mats. The Zogui

* See Appendix, VIII: "The Trial of Poison."

pronounces the sacramental words, brandishing his trident: "Now you are Toma." Then messengers are sent off to announce to the women that their children have been devoured by the Great Spirit, and that they will see them again, safe and sound, when they have been digested and ejected.

The tattooing is not without danger: the same knife and the same thorn serve for several children, and are not disinfected. The witch-doctors daub the cuts with a medicine of their own compounding, derived from cow dung; often it transforms simple cuts into suppurating wounds. Toma powers of resistance generally overcome the infection. The cure requires about a month, during which time the children are forbidden to bathe or to engage in any strenuous activity.

The mark of the Afwi has the form of a band of vertical, raised welts, starting at the points of the breasts and swinging under the arms in a wide loop that rises between the shoulder-blades to the nape of the neck.

An occasional neophyte succumbs following his initiation, but these are exceptional cases, and Zézé enjoyed great prestige: during the seven tattooing ceremonies he had conducted, no child had died.

These rites, seemingly so barbarous, can be rationalized in terms of the Toma way of life. During his first two years the Toma baby never leaves his mother's back. He participates without knowing it in all village activities—dances, work in the fields—but as soon as he is old enough to walk, he finds himself alone. He eats and sleeps when he wants to, plays with his friends, wanders in the forest, and observes none of the prohibitions usually imposed on little European boys. It is a curious fact that very few accidents occur during this period.

But in the eyes of the tribe the boy is asexual; he has not yet become a part of the community. At puberty he must die as a child to be reborn a man, conscious of his rights and of his duties toward others. Stripping away any mythical trappings, the initiation clearly marks a true transformation. It obliges the young boy to cast out the terrors of childhood, and demands of him a greater resistance to pain. But the ordeal in itself would be insufficient if a long stay in the forest were not added to it. The child now knows the great secrets of his tribe, but he is not capable of the man's full part, cannot yet stand up to life in the bush. He must learn all that was useful and necessary to the Toma before the white man came.

First the boys construct a small village within the initiation camp —as they will later construct huts for themselves and their families. They clear strips for farming, sow and reap their own rice, pick coconuts and express oil from them, and soon learn to identify all the forest's edible fruit, to follow the spoor of game, and to hunt with dogs. They weave their own cotton for tunics, and in their leisure time they braid rope. Any surplus products are distributed among their relatives.

Aside from that purely material education, the witch-doctors stress all the great tribal traditions: the names of forest spirits and of heroes; the concoction of medicine and poisons; the interpretation of the spirits' will by the fall of kola nuts; the reading of omens during sacrifices; taboos; and the ritual of high ceremony.

The art of communication through sound occupies an important position in the curriculum. We knew, for example, that the Toma could transmit any message by tom-tom or whistle. We had learned this the year before, in a rather curious way: after recording the bird-men, who danced to the accompaniment of a tiny wooden drum, we had run back the tape for the whole population of Niogbozu. At several points they broke into laughter for no apparent reason. Suspecting the reason, we had run it through again. They laughed at the same spots. That evening I asked our interpreter, Prosper Zumanigui, to explain all the hilarity.

"The tom-toms were making jokes. The Toma make tom-toms talk. It's like the soldier's bugle—when it blows, they all know right away whether it's dinner time or someone wants the top sergeant."

The children learn still another essential art: how to make the Afwi speak. The performance of sacred music follows a very precise ritual; the artists are allowed no personal interpretation, and they are trained to the ritual during their stay in the bush. Incidentally, Toma music, sacred or profane, seems to be the monopoly of a few privileged artists. Small orchestras, like the one that had accompanied us through the bush, cover the countryside like troubadours, showing up at every important ceremony and following the higher dignitaries in their travels.

Within the initiation camp the Wenilegagui, charged with the enforcement of tribal law, punish any infraction even more severely than in the villages. The child, when he leaves, must be automatically and instinctively respectful of tradition. He is tied to his tribe by common secrets, and must contribute, in all his activities, to the maintenance of ancestral custom and to the well-being of the community. In compensation he can count on the community's support and can unload some of his responsibilities on it. From time to time he undergoes new physical trials: abandoned in the forest, for example, he must keep alive with no help from anyone.

The initiation period can last for seven years. At its end the boys go back to the family hut. One of the great Toma celebrations takes place on this occasion. The return of the initiates attracts an even greater crowd than the tattooing, being the occasion of sumptuous feasting and dancing.

The ceremony begins with a sort of baptism, which takes place within the confines of the forest, and which only initiates may witness. The child takes a purifying bath in the river, lying with his head upstream. The witch-doctor, in his incantations, then confirms the secret name given the boy during his initiation, and the name is echoed by tom-toms or flutes. The boy is then led to a magic barrier that he must cross in one leap, in the presence of dignitaries; seven different leaves have been dispersed among those already on the ground across the barrier, and he must not touch any of the seven. He has nothing but luck to help him, but this is one of the risks of life: the Toma do not like unlucky men.

At dawn on the day of the return, a messenger enters the village and smashes an earthenware vessel at the doorsill of any family whose son has died during the initiation, saying: "Your son is like this vessel." The relatives may not show their sorrow until after the ceremony, and must participate in all the rejoicing. The father may have known the facts previously, having been permitted to enter the initiation camp occasionally; but bound to secrecy, he had not the right to tell his wife.

During his stay in the bush, Zézé's elder son was killed in a fall from a palm tree, and the grand master of the witch-doctors had never let the slightest bitterness show.

An esplanade extended before the entrance to the sacred wood, like a stage upon which the witch-doctors would give astounding proof of their magical powers. One by one, the vegetation and the most dangerous animals of the bush obeyed their commands. It had taken us a good while to dig clarification of this out of Voiné. "The trees move," he had said, "and the animals come when the witch-doctors call." But now we bore Afwi's mark on our backs, and Voiné could speak out.

In reality, only a few thin and flexible tree-trunks moved at the Zogui's command. A young boy, ensconced at the top of a stripped trunk, as on a stilt, and masked by a fringe of raffia, made the trunk oscillate in all directions. The bush animals made their presence known mainly by their cries, and the most feared of all, the panthers, were nothing more than initiates sewn into skins, who imitated the animals' movements perfectly, at least when seen from a distance. Then a dignitary advanced to the gateway of the sacred wood and demanded of the Afwi, through the thick fern roots, the boys of the village. A long dialogue ensued. The Afwi required sacrifices in return for the boys. All the villagers came nearer; gifts were heaped up; and the children at last came out of their isolation.

Dances followed, starring all the personalities of the sacred wood, and the celebration ended with a gigantic meal, at which the sacrificed animals were eaten.

An analogous symbolism is found in all initiations. Before being incorporated into the group, the postulant must submit to a series of psychological and physical trials that plunge him into a second state, comparable to dying, and bring him forth again into consciousness as a new man.

The differences in ritual between entry and exit seem very significant in this respect. At the beginning the child is exposed to a direct and brutal revelation of the Afwi in all his power. The Great Spirit is a manifestation of the union of all the Toma, and in the course of that first ceremony the combined psychic force of all the region's witch-doctors confers an unusual reality upon him. When the young man leaves the forest, on the other hand, he participates in the magic himself, instead of submitting to it. The witch-doctors prove their confidence in him by asking his complicity in a demonstration of their power.

According to Voiné, the Kissi, neighbors of the Toma, paid very dearly for the secrets of tattooing, because among primitives everywhere the same rites exist under slightly different aspects, and their aim is to assure the continuance of tradition, and of tradition's corollary, the pre-eminence of the community over the individual. One vital necessity brings men together in their fight for life against a hostile forest; and their collectivity must reject inept or inefficient members. A sizeable infant mortality operates a preliminary natural selection; the stay in the forest, through its rigor, imposes a second elimination.

It was astonishing to see that among the Toma circumcision, held indispensable, nevertheless played no important role in the initiation. It seemed to be a physiological necessity, and no special rite marked it. If you want to be circumcised," Voiné told us, "it will cost one sheep for the four of you; you already owe us a bull, because we tattooed your backs. Or you could become Guelemlai."

We hadn't considered this commercial aspect of the question. Now we saw the origins of the messengers of the sacred wood: they were, in general, children of poor families, unable to afford the great tattooing; those who, in Voiné's terms, "had very hard hearts." Sent to the witch-doctors by their parents two years before the date set, they passed through the ritual ordeal, had their heads shaved, were painted with lime and dressed in the raffia horse-collar, and then traveled through the region preparing the initiation of their former playmates.

"When the Guelemlai come to Tuwelu, then the Soguru ceremony will be all ready to exist," Voiné said.

Would the incisions be healed over in time? It was our only worry. Cloistered in the green shadows of our small clearing, we spent most of our time stretched in our hammocks, sleeping or chatting. Daylight filtered over us through the arch of giant trees. Now and then little gray or brown monkeys flew from liana to liana and watched us from a distance. Close by, the waterfall rumbled; we could not even go to bathe.

Voiné brought us all our meals, and usually stayed with us until dark. Often Wego came with him. Much more loquacious than before the tattooing, they went on answering all our questions freely; so we learned how a man became a witch-doctor.

He had to be predestined to it. Actually he did not become, but was born, a witch-doctor. At his birth the women, by signs known to them only, of which Voiné himself was ignorant, designated the child who would later be capable of fulfilling the witch-doctor's function. Beginning at that moment, certain precautions were taken. As soon as he could walk, the child was exiled from his family's village, and from his father in particular, and confided to a Zogui, who began the child's education well before the tattooing.

Having gone through the same ordeal as the others, the future witch-doctor continued his study of magic and ritual, under the direction of his master. Then he had to give proof of his gifts. According to Voiné, he went through no supplementary physical trials. His examinations bore most strongly on intuition and astuteness; and our guide told us how he himself had passed the last tests.

The witch-doctors of his village, assembled in the sacred wood, had chosen among themselves one of nine balls of rice placed on a flat rock in the center of the clearing. Voiné, called up, had to find it without hesitation and eat it: the others were poisoned.

The witch-doctor, once confirmed in his position, became the guardian of tradition and of all the tribal secrets. Voiné had often spoken to us of "wizards," but now we understand that he used the word in a pejorative sense, applying it to the inferior witch-doctors who were Zézé's enemies.

All witch-doctors had assistants; it was curious, but the soothsayer Wego, in spite of his position and his advanced age, was only Zézé's right-hand man.

"And I, still very young," Voiné added, "I can give orders to almost all the elders of Tuwelu, because I'm going to replace Zézé when he dies."

The assistant's functions were well defined. He replaced the Zogui in all operations prohibited to a man of the Zogui's high rank, and could, when necessary, take responsibility for doing away with his master's enemies.

"If we want to, we can drive a man crazy in a few weeks," Wego confirmed, when we consulted him.

I thought back to our sleepless nights, to the strange sounds, the inexplicable music, the two or three Voinés. What reactions might a similarly jittery atmosphere produce in a man who had been buried since childhood in the magical climate of the forest?

I opened one eye. Voiné was leaning over me and shaking my hammock.

"Let's go, *patron*. On your feet."

Day had barely broken. Voiné would never lose that habit of waking us too early. Wego had come with him; he watched Tony, who was crawling painfully out of bed.

"The master will wash you in the river," Voiné said. "Then you'll be free."

He had doubtless taken that decision with Zézé the night before, after an examination of our scars, but he had said nothing at the time. We had been prisoners in our well of greenery for almost a week and would be happy to be at liberty again.

We were up to our waists in the eddying current. It was chill in the early morning shadows. Roosting on a boulder across from us, Wego screamed incantations that were lost in the roar of the waterfall, and sprayed us with handfuls of leaves. Impassive, arms folded, Voiné observed us from the bank.

After this ritual baptism we stepped out of the water, shivering, and dried ourselves half-heartedly with cautious movements. The swollen incisions around the ribs still stung.

Then, with our bedrolls made up, we hit the trail to the village.

An unaccustomed order prevailed in our hut. During our absence Voiné had cleaned house with great care. He must have been bored with leisure, to undertake the job. We gave him a vote of thanks.

We were just settled again when an old man, trembling all over, came to search us out. He extracted a sheet of printed matter from the pocket of his tunic and handed it to me. A former soldier, he knew a few words of French, but he had never learned to read; and in our absence no one had been able to decipher the disturbing message. A quick explanation transformed his worry into delirous joy: he was to report to the military post in Macenta, to pick up pension arrears.

As he left we saw Zézé approaching, his expression sad. There must have been bad news. He sat under the awning, slumped and discouraged: the tattooing at Soguru, which was supposed to take place in a few days, had just been postponed. It was impossible to wheedle more information on this subject from our witch-doctors. They had some vague notion of what a week was, having followed the example of their neighbors, the Moslemized Malinké, whose day of rest was Saturday, but the Toma had substituted Friday. According to Voiné, a few of the very old men still remembered the highly elastic ten months that made up the Toma year. But actually it was only the cycle of seasons and the work in the *lugans* that marked the passage of time for them. By successive approximations we finally understood that we were condemned to almost a whole month of waiting.

Since our arrival the celebration of that rite had been postponed repeatedly. Were Zézé's witch-doctor enemies fighting a war of attrition?

Grayish cloud-banks invaded the still-blue morning sky. A diluvian rain swept down on the village. During our six days in the bush not a drop of rain had fallen. This time Voiné had been right: the Okobuzogui had protected us while we were unsheltered.

A few hours later old Voiné Beawogui showed up. He had just come back from a trip through the Soguru region, and confirmed Zézé's reports. The tattooing had been set for the first quarter of the next moon, or in about a month. Our pessimistic suppositions were also correct: the witch-doctors in Soguru feared our presence, and in order to avoid it had resolved to wait until the last possible moment, in the hope of seeing us leave before.

"I don't bother with their magic affairs," old Voiné added, "but I know something about this. They won't be able to postpone things again, and when the dirty weather sets in before the rainy season

151

they'll have to go through with it or the ancestors' spirits will be angry and they'll all die."

This extra delay upset our plans again. The early rainy season was beginning, and we were afraid that humidity might spoil the film we had already shot. It ought to be sent off to France right away, but it would have to be accompanied. Virel volunteered for the mission. Regret was evident on his face. He would leave the next day. We would go along to Bofosso with him.

That night our witch-doctor friends came to share our meal. Voiné confirmed the invitation extended by the district chief, Koli Zumanigui, whom we had met at Foromo's place in Macenta. We were invited to the women's high ceremony; it was to take place about now in Koli's village. There, perhaps, we could film more secret rites. This made Virel's sacrifice even more painful, and at the sight of his distress the witch-doctors insisted on offering him a gift; it would prove everywhere, even in France, that the Toma thought of him as a brother. Wego gave him a broad-striped tunic, Voiné a miniature of the mask of Angbai, and Zézé a witch-doctor's trident.

Wenilegagui, the bird-man, in full ceremonial dress.

Laniboi, the dancer on stilts.

photo by F

The female Bakorogui, a ritual mask.

Voiné Koiwogui, guide, interpreter, witch-doctor, loyal friend.

Angbai, the bush-devil. Mask belonging to Voiné Koiwogui, and used by him in the performance of secret personal rites.

oto by Saulnier

Trial of a thief in Bofosso. When apprehended, he was carrying a thief's protective charms; there was no doubt of his guilt. The cords on his arms were bound tightly while wet. As they dried they caused excruciating pain, forcing him to confess.

Vuriakoli with Gaisseau at the Baluma Mission. A powerful and obstinate witch-doctor, he was an unyielding obstacle to the expedition.

photo by Saulni

Jean Fichter crossing the bridge of liana vines over the Boyda River.

photo by Saulnier

Zézé Sohowogui, master witch-doctor, who threw his intelligence, courage, and influence on the side of the expedition. The trident is the symbol of his authority. BELOW: Wego, the soothsayer. Older than Zézé, he was nevertheless Zézé's assistant, as witch-doctors outranked soothsayers.

photo by Saulnier

A young woman painting on the wall of a hut in Doezia.

The convention area in Doezia.

Pallbearers carrying an old woman to her grave.

Votive offerings at an ancestral tomb.

photo by Sa

Too old and feeble to hunt or farm, he stays behind in the village.

Slaughter of a sacrificial bull in Tuwelu.

photo by Sau

Carrying away a trophy after the sacrifice of the bull.

Interior of the medicine hut. AT LEFT, Vollolibei, the female fetish of Tuwelu.

photo by Saul

Wego, the soothsayer, could not conduct rites, but set dates for them and foretold the future. Here he uses beans, stones, and kola nuts in prophesying about the conspiracy against Zézé.

Okobuzogui, half ram and half crocodile, secret
incarnation of the Afwi, or Great Spirit.

Zézé in the Sacred Wood, about to sacrifice his dog.

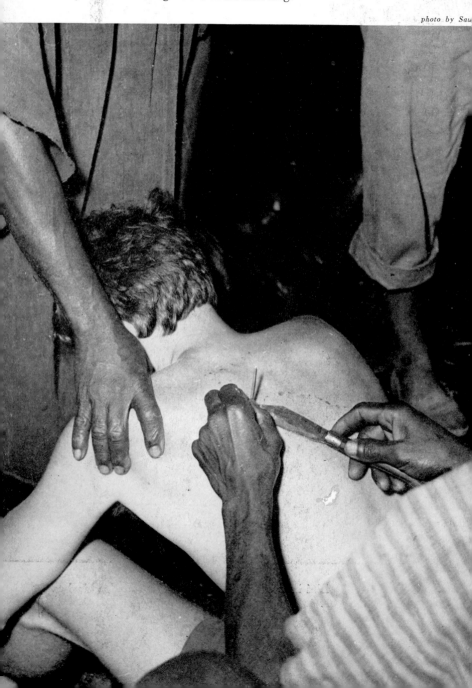

After the tattooing, Fichter, Gaisseau, and Virel
are baptized in the river of the Sacred Wood.

A quiet hour in the Sacred Wood, while the tattooed men
recuperate. LEFT, Virel; RIGHT. Gaisseau.

Young excised girls returning from the Sacred Wood of women.

photo by Saulnier

The initiates surround Voiné; he must offer them a gift for his freedom.

Celebration of the female initiates' return: an initiate
dances accompanied by an orchestra of native maracas.

photo by Saul

An excised girl, suddenly unveiled by the wind, protects herself against the evil spells of the photographer.

Symbolic war dance celebrating the return of the women from initiation rites.

photo by Sauln

The infirmary. Even the children were docile patients.

The Guelemlai, forest messengers, at the entrance to the initiation forest.

photo by Saul

The Guelemlai come to round up the candidates for initiation.

Zézé, upon hearing that he will be tried for sacrilege.

photo by Saul

Okobuzogui again: the secret incarnation of the Afwi, or Great Spirit.

NINE

With an agonized clash of gears, the truck taking Virel to Macenta shot off; it disappeared quickly behind its own cloud of dust. We were back in the small hut across from Baré's *gargote*, and we had the painful feeling that we were starting again from scratch. We were a little worried about our families' reactions when Virel turned up alone. In spite of all the explanatory letters we had loaded him with, we knew that there would be strenuous objections on their part to this new and indefinite delay.

The coalition of hostile witch-doctors was not disarming. Zézé and Voiné alluded to it in every conversation; but confident of their power since they had made initiates of us, they had no fears for their final success.

"The conspiracy will be broken up," Voiné repeated. "You're not Bilakoro now. You're Toma."

And still stubborn, he began to prepare for our trip into the Baezia district. In Koli he saw a powerful potential ally; he did not want to lose a moment in acting on the invitation. He had already found a native trucker who would take us up the Kissidugu road to its meeting with the trail to Bueylazu, where the district chief lived. That way we would have no need of porters; there would remain only a couple of miles to cover on foot, and Koli could send his men for the equipment.

We reached Bueylazu in the morning, under a cloudless sky. A

THE SACRED FOREST

153

colorful, chattering crowd filled the village square. The village was as animated as Bofosso on market day. Zézé and Voiné led us through the crowd toward Koli Zumanigui's large hut; its corrugated-iron roof glittered in the sunlight.

The district chief of Baezia was a considerable personality. With his innumerable family he occupied almost the whole of the village. The tomb of his ancestors was of cement. He possessed over two hundred wives, a phonograph, a new bicycle, and a dilapidated Matford that lay under a kind of carport built out from the hut's awning. At his doorsill he greeted us amiably. He wore a soft felt hat, a flowered sport shirt à la California, and a pair of shorts.

"*Iche . . . icheyo . . . imama . . . mamayo.*"

Then he asked us in.

An enormous table surrounded by massive, locally manufactured armchairs took up half the reception room; the room's walls were white and bare. Without stopping, he led us into the second room, furnished with two beds.

"Here you are at home," he said.

Settled down in the larger room, around the immense table (which had a meat-grinder permanently bolted to it), we chatted, drinking red wine out of various receptacles.

"Koli knows that you're tattooed and that you know the Toma secrets," Voiné said.

Koli nodded approval with a wide smile.

A small woman, frail, thin-faced, entered with supple dancing steps.

"That's Voru, one of Koli's best wives."

She went to Zézé; they touched hands, slapping lightly with their fingertips. Voru was the old witch-doctor's daughter; but he had changed his name upon arrival. Here he was no longer called Zézé, but Vorukaya: the father of Voru.

Koli explained that he had assigned Voru to our service. She smiled pleasantly and left on light feet.

Then I noticed a large woman with light skin, draped in wide folds of blue satin. Standing in a corner, she watched us, motionless, her eyes empty. She had probably emerged from a room opposite ours, where our host slep in his canopied bed. Koli seemed to ignore her presence.

I threw a questioning look at Voiné.

"That's the sacrifice-wife," he said.

"The sacrifice-wife?"

All the great chiefs had one wife more fair-skinned than the others. It was forbidden to beat them or to become angry at them.

"Do you know why?"

"That's just the way it is. Or if you beat her, you have to make a sacrifice. And she never works!"

All through our stay with Koli we would see that statue wander empty-handed about the house, or stand leaning against a door-jamb, or sit mute in an armchair hours on end.

The ceremony to which Koli Zumanigui had invited us was a return-from-excision celebration. Voiné explained the rites at great length. Women too have their talismans and their sacred wood, neighboring that of the men; there the girls undergo excision. That sexual mutilation is performed by matrons of the village under the direction of female witch-doctors. After excision the girls spend a period of two years in the bush, during which time they learn what every Toma woman must know in order to play her proper part in the community. Finally, on a day set by the matrons, they return to the village, where ceremonies performed in their honor take place.

No Toma ceremony could begin without the ritual exchange of presents. Koli Zumanigui, in a pith helmet, seated among the dignitaries on a folding chair in the shadow of his hut, received his gifts with great dignity. One by one the women detached themselves from the assembled crowd, bearing on their heads huge bundles of *guinzé*, basins of rice or pimento, gourds of palm oil, rolls of cotton cloth. Little by little the pile of gifts grew at Koli's feet.

Each of the women was escorted by a dignitary, who commented until he was breathless on the importance and value of the offerings.

Koli listened with a resigned expression, gave brief thanks, and proceeded to redistribute the gifts among the spectators. Certain of them, reserved for the returning girls, were immediately carried off to the women's sacred wood.

Voiné and Zézé, side by side, watched, listened, and approved, tirelessly.

For two days we suffered these punctilious preliminaries.

The sun was setting. From the near-by forest rose a chant at once religious and savage, the like of which we had never heard before. Out of a lane between two huts surged a dense cortege of women, advancing into the village to the rhythm of maracas. Breasts high, hands at their sides, they paraded around the square with dragging steps. Now and then their chorus broke off, their palms lifted toward the skies, and a long, screeching clamor rose, tearing at our ear-drums. Above the moving column oscillated two long, thin figures, borne at arm's length and veiled in white cotton.

"The first one," Voiné said, "is the Zazi, the medicine of all women. The other is a female witch-doctor rolled up in a mat like a corpse."

The matrons of excision brought up the rear. Their hips bound in their most handsome loincloths, high truncated bonnets on their heads, bonnets striped in lively colors, they shuffled a vague dance-step and brandished long tongs and knives, the attributes of their function. Under the gaze of the attentive crowd they mimed, with cheerful sadism, the gestures of the operation.

Beside the line of march a slim-waisted woman in an *m'bila* capered hilariously; she seemed to be leading the parade. Slung on her shoulders were a rosary of sheep's shoulder-blades and bunches of toucans' beaks; she was frantically waving a large rotten banana.

We wanted to start shooting; I took a step forward. But Voiné held me back: no man could approach the cortege. When I insisted, he showed me an enormous old woman sitting under the awning of a hut, between two particularly grim-looking matrons. "You'll have to go ask her."

"Her" was the most important female witch-doctor in the region. This whole ceremony had required her authorization. She could have stopped it dead with a single gesture. She must have weighed close to four hundred pounds. A little while before, I had seen her cross the square. Unable to stand erect, she could walk only by pushing a sort of wooden roller in front of her.

"To carry her through the bush she needs twenty porters," Voiné said, full of admiration.

The Toma believed that it never rained when she was traveling, but that the sky became cloudy, to spare her the crushing heat.

I hesitated a moment and then started toward her, with Voiné at my side. She turned her bloated face to me and gave me a single crushing glance. In the hope of winning her over, I had Voiné deliver our gift. This once, at least, our interpreter would have been happy to pass up the intermediary's role. The woman paid no attention to his speech and threw the bills in my face. Then she turned her back on us. Voiné glanced at me with worried eyes. I had another argument in reserve. Voiné translated:

"I know that you have no need of this money. You command all the women of the region, and during this celebration even the men. I beg you to accept, in all friendship, a bottle of rum we had brought along for ourselves."

The metamorphosis was instantaneous. Was she aware that we were depriving ourselves of a very precious commodity? Her whole face lit up; she took my hands, and had Voiné tell me that we were friends.

"You can take pictures, but not too close up."

In the square the women's dance continued. Finally, after a last shout, they started back along the trail to the forest.

"It's not over," Voiné said, seeing me start to break down the equipment. "It gets even better now. *Formidable!*"

Voiné was fond of that comprehensive adjective, an enrichment of his vocabulary he owed to us, and he used it as correctly as most whites. This time he might be perfectly accurate. Unfortunately, the sun was dropping fast behind the forest, and in a few minutes it would be too late to shoot.

"Absolutely *formidable!* You'll see," Voiné repeated impatiently; he had always refused to reckon with technical requirements.

A heavy stamping of feet, like the steps of a giant animal, shook the village. Two white masts, some thirty feet high, rose above the conical roofs; bright pennants streamed from them. Another parade emerged from the lane. Two groups of women alternately raised and let fall the heavy masts. Only this dull pounding accompanied the women's chant. Among the paraders were many in pointed, black, horned headdresses: these were the *excisées;* as Voiné put it, the *exquises*.

Oncoming night blotted out most of the details. Now the square was only a dark, writhing human mass, whirling endlessly to the same haunting music. Against the last light of day, only the two tall masts and the initiates' headdresses stood out.

We had filmed the greater part of the ceremony. Tonight all we could do was record the women's chants.

The generator was outside the circle of lianas, at the end of a hundred yards of cable: this arrangement cut out machine static. Tony and Jean took a lantern and went to start it up. I stayed behind

CHAPTER NINE

159

at the tape recorder. A few inquisitive people made a circle around me. Ten minutes went by; the pilot bulb above my head had not so much as flashed. There was a bug somewhere. I went to join Jean and Tony, leaving Voiné to watch over the equipment.

We had set the generator on a platform of earth, to keep it from being drowned in the rain. Sitting on the thick trunk of a felled tree, Jean and Tony, visibly wearied, were catching their breath. For ten minutes they had been pulling vainly on the starter-lanyard. I tried it myself, with no success. Jean pushed me aside authoritatively.

"Wait a minute," he said. "Don't wear yourself out. I'll try it again, three times. If nothing happens we'll strip it down."

After the three pulls we got to work on the mechanism. We cleaned the parts carefully and spread them out on a tarp. We tried to eliminate all possible causes of breakdown. Then a discussion arose over the best procedure in reassembly. Jean won. When the last bolt had been tightened, the machine looked the way it always had. But it was wasted effort. The motor would not respond.

We were sitting there discouraged when our three witch-doctors came up silently; if anything, they were more upset than we.

"Koli and all the villagers are waiting for the machine," Voiné said, with a shade of rebuke in his voice.

In those few words he gave us to understand that our prestige was frittering away by the minute. Jean got busy again and in his nervousness broke the lanyard. Tony replaced him—and bruised his hand badly. I tried a few times, failing, and then slid on the muddy slope and landed hard.

"Wait," Voiné said. "I'll do it."

But he had no success and was soon discouraged.

Zézé, who had been squatting in the shadows until then, rose and without a word wrapped the lanyard around the wheel. We tried to make him understand that his efforts were futile, but he waved us off. His advanced age allowed him only feeble and fruitless motions. He got tangled up in his full tunic, displaced the generator on its platform, and ended by breaking the lanyard again. For an instant he stared at the machine scornfully; then he gestured, and Wego and Voiné followed him into the forest.

Left alone, we tinkered with the motor, not too hopefully. Over in the village the chants had ceased, and we decided to give up, at least for tonight. We had begun to pack the tools when the witch-doctors appeared again.

"Now it'll work," Voiné said confidently. "We just made a sacrifice."

Without much conviction we tried again. Not even a sputter.

"I'm going to tighten the spark-plugs," Jean said. "I did it once a little while ago, but you never know."

Two minutes and he was finished; on the first try the motor coughed; on the second it caught with a weird noise and finally roared to life. Jean, who had been leaning over it, nursing it, stood up with a grin of triumph. Zézé and Voiné, of course, were smiling. Each had perfectly good reasons to take credit for the success.

A noisy crowd had invaded Koli's hut, and we had trouble getting through to the recorder. Electric bulbs were plugged into the motor; their light was harsh.

The natives all wanted to listen, and no one would sing; in spite of Voiné's laborious explanations they had not yet understood too well what it was that we wanted of them. Koli volunteered first to deliver a speech into the microphone. Then he cleared away a large semicircle in front of the loudspeaker hung above the door and came to stand in the center. Shouts of enthusiasm greeted the play-back of his voice, and the women began suddenly to sing. We recorded for more than a quarter of an hour, and when the time came to play it all back, Koli, who had turned out to be a conscientious sergeant-at-arms, brought the female witch-doctors and the matrons of excision to the first row of auditors. Jean turned up the amplifier to its maximum, and the music roared out louder than nature. The terrified old women almost stampeded; but kept in place by the crowd, they gradually lost their fear, finally laughing at themselves and coming up to thank us. Koli seemed very satisfied with the demonstration.

"Tomorrow," he said, "I'll send for the Orapossu tom-toms, and you can record the best of Toma music."

It was still darkest night when Voiné, who had been sleeping on a mat in the reception room, came into the bedroom—earlier than ever.

"Today the women will bring their secrets back into the village. No man is permitted to go outside. You're like us now. When the women begin, you close the door, and you won't try to spy on them."

We promised readily enough, flattered that we had been assimilated to the Toma.

With the first light of dawn a distant chant, very slow, reached us from the forest and approached rapidly; suddenly a deafening clamor surrounded us, one word repeated endlessly: *"Sao! . . . Sao! . . ."* ("Death! . . . Death!")

"The women are naked," Voiné said, "and they're carrying their fetish around the village."

That was all he knew. What the fetish was, no man could have told us.

We stepped into the large room. Koli and his friends were assembled around the table. They seemed impressed by these funereal cries. Melancholy, they drank wine, pouring it from demijohn to coffeepot and from coffeepot to cup. Koli filled goblets for us. The corrosive liquid had an aftertaste of crude oil, and we absorbed it without pleasure, our eyes carefully and ostentatiously directed at the blank wall: we could easily have looked out on the square through cracks in the rotting door, but we were Toma now and respected the ritual.

For about two hours the women went on howling at death and parading through the village.

Abruptly the chorus was stilled; a few moments later we were authorized to go outside. Medieval specters flitted through the village: the excised women, in their high pointed headdresses, faces hidden behind white veils, were hurrying back to the women's sacred wood to prepare themselves. Now it was time to celebrate: all the men would have the right to join the dance, and we would be able to film whatever we wanted to.

Feverishly we set up the camera and accessories at a strategic point where we would lose nothing of the ceremonies; and we waited there alone for an hour. Voiné had disappeared. Finally, tired of waiting, we broke down the equipment, and just as we turned toward our hut, the first shots rang out and the maraca orchestra broke into rhythm. Voiné appeared on the doorsill of our hut.

"Quick, *patron*. It's beginning."

"Don't run away now," I said to him. "We'll need an interpreter all the time."

We set up our equipment again and were ready for the excised women. They came out of the forest in single file. Dense fringes of black cotton thread hung from their headpieces, veiling their faces and forcing them to walk with their heads bowed. Their only clothing was a blue or white loincloth edged, like the headpiece, with long fringes of cotton. Their bodies were covered with bold black ritual paintings similar to those on the huts; bracelets of panthers' teeth, tinkling bells, and assorted charms completed their ornamentation. Some of them wore, as a pendant, a kind of cross, of which the vertical member was somewhat rounded. I pointed one out to Voiné. "What's that?"

"Can't you tell?" he said, laughing. "That's a Toma airplane!"

I thought he was joking.

"No, no," he said. "The airplane is good medicine."

The excised women approached the village square in a rocking shuffle. Some twenty old women were waiting for them, beating out a rhythm with maracas the size of pumpkins; the maracas were wrapped in nets, and the links of the nets were decorated with monkeys' vertebræ. The sudden deafening rattle of these giant maracas evoked the rapid puffing of a locomotive more than anything else; the chants were hardly audible. The roar of guns echoed on all sides. The chants were lost, overwhelmed in the tumult. The excised women prostrated themselves toward the orchestra, faces to earth, in one long rank, and then rose slowly. With the elegant gestures of their arms, panther-teeth bracelets clattered. Then the women stood and separated, and each danced alone, surrounded by a group of spectators. They seemed to follow their own inspiration; hieratic poses, recalling Far Eastern dance figures, followed suddenly upon rapid, complicated native steps.

On a woman's gleaming back, just below the waist, I noticed several ribbons of deeply scarred tattooing.

"That's only to make them pretty," Voiné explained. "For women the tattooing that counts is the excision."

"But those beauty marks must be a lot more painful than the men's."

"Absolutely," he said, "but they don't know it, and the important thing is not to tell them."

The men came one by one to dance before the girls and set gifts at their feet; matrons gathered up the presents immediately. Now and then a hunter would snuggle the butt of his rifle against a girl's shoulder and fire into the air. He had offered her that powder charge.

When the men's generosity slowed, the excised girls suddenly surrounded a young man; he had to make them a gift or flee into the bush. The ring-around-a-rosy technique was part of the game.

CHAPTER NINE

165

I found it very funny until it was turned against me. Lassoed by a liana lariat fringed with raffia, I had to dance for my freedom—not forgetting the ritual gift, of course.

The orchestra of maracas stopped occasionally to give the girls time to catch their breath. But the young women were forbidden to sit on the ground. Two women sat back against a hut and extended their legs, across which the initiate could lie while other women sheltered her from the sun and fanned her by flapping cloths.

"Those are the husband's other wives," Voiné said.

I learned then that most of the girls were destined to their future husbands even before they entered the forest, and that their parents had already received the marriage portion.

Koli pedaled peacefully out of the lane between two huts on his new bicycle and came to sit beside us. It was his first appearance of the day. In his honor the dances started up again, and young girls came to prostrate themselves before him.

"Six of them are for me," he confided.

"Six out of twenty-three, and you already have more than two hundred."

"A man never has enough. The more wives you have, the more power you have, and the fewer plots against you."

Then he pointed out a small bearded man in shorts, a pith helmet, and hobnailed boots; we had already singled him out for his unstinting vigor at dancing, and because he was throwing away a king's ransom on presents.

"See him? That's my brother. He wanted to take my place. He and the others plotted against me for six years, but it's all well in hand now. . . . There's always a lot of that among the Toma, but if you can take care of yourself it's not serious. *Yes sir!*"

"Do you speak English?"

"I lived in Liberia for six years."

Voiné was right. We would probably find a valuable ally in Koli.

Out of the apparent chaos of the celebration the theme of the dancing gradually became clearer. The excised women, alone or in groups, were miming the principal tribal activities. One of them flailed the air with two wooden sabers, one green and the other red, imitating men at war; another, with a broom of palm leaves, was dusting and tidying the hut; others, hunched forward, were weeding *lugans,* or, basins in hand, preparing dinner. In the ballet movement that followed I recognized parodies of special events—for example, a visit by the district chief. A girl wearing a full embroidered tunic and a red turban over her pointed hat made a tour of the huts, followed by all the others, who portrayed the chief's wives. The favorite, whose hand rested on the "husband's" shoulder, rapidly gave way to each of the others in turn.

Two of the excised women, their faces still hidden by the black fringe of their hats, stepped into the square. They were costumed, one in an impeccable white suit, the other in a short and stylish European dress. Voiné nudged me.

"Those are *wigui,*" he said.

I looked ignorant.

"The *wigui* are the whites. It means 'heavy,' like rocks—those who can't be moved."

I had no trouble recognizing the caricature of a district commander and his wife in the gait and gestures of the dancers. The girl playing a man's part even had a pencil and a notebook and scribbled away tirelessly: writing, to the Toma, was the most astonishing of all the white man's activities. A table and chairs were brought to the dancers; the man continued to scribble while he collected taxes that the other dancers set before him. The taxpayers were flanked by two girls carrying imitation swagger-sticks, who represented the sergeants-at-arms.

"They imitate the whites well," I said to Voiné.

"Yes, they're real *wigui*. . . . And do you know what they call you, the four of you?"

"No."

"The *wigui-wigui*."

"Why?"

"Because you always do just what you want to. Nobody can change your minds about anything. You've seen all the secrets."

In a moment of relative calm we sat down in the shade. The dances seemed to have brought Voiné to a high pitch of excitement.

"I don't understand—" he began.

We all looked at him.

"—how you can go without a woman for so long. A Toma couldn't. . . ."

"What do you suggest?" Tony said.

"You ought to revolutionize an initiate."

The meaning of that last linguistic innovation was clear, but we had no desire to explain that, aside from any personal reasons, we wanted to take no chances with the always lively sensitivity of the Toma.

"We don't even know how to tell them what we want."

"I can't do it for you," Voiné said. "Here among the Toma there's no such thing as a pander. If you want a woman, you have to arrange things yourself. It's easy; you say: *iba ga we*. They understand right away. That means: 'You're pretty.' . . ."

Voiné went on with a lesson in the vocabulary of the gallant.

"Put it all down, now," he said suddenly and sternly. "You'll forget."

And on the margin of a sheet of ethnographic notes, we took down his dictation of a series of ingenuous and direct questions and answers.

———

In a little courtyard within a low stone wall behind Koli's hut I escaped the throng for a while; the singing and the ratttle of maracas were slightly deadened, and I could try to make sense of the whole celebration.

That morning the secret procession of the women, comparable to the ritual of the Afwi, had been a revelation to me. The women too, then, were organized in an occult society with a hierarchy parallel to the men's. But while the Afwi seemed to stand for the life-force of the Toma and the forest, the women invoked death. Their magic involved no terrifying masks; no guardian of the portal, no symbolic gateway, distinguished their sacred wood from the surrounding bush. Even in public ceremonies their talismans emerged veiled, while the Vollolibei, for example, could be looked upon by all during the parade through the village. Excision was the true initiation rite for these girls, and tattooing only an æsthetic expression; yet among the males circumcision was motivated by physiological necessities alone, and only the tattooing could transform a young boy into a man. The men's magic manifested its power constantly through external signs. The women's magic developed discreetly, in shadow. What could be seen was of small importance to them.

So two complementary universes stood revealed. This dualism was evident in most Toma rites. The sole symbol of Creation, the "thunderstone," was called *Zazi* or *Belimassai*, depending on whether men or women spoke of it. To the *bakorozine* (literally, "man-body"), guardian of the sacred wood, corresponded the *bakorozai*, the "woman-body." During this initiation festival the female Vollolibei of Tuwelu joined the male of a near-by village.

Even earlier, among the Piaroa of the Orinoco, I had noticed that sacred music was performed on two groups of almost identical instruments, flutes and horns of slightly different size, called male or female by the Indians.

That initial differentiation of the sexes, which seems common to most primitive communities, naturally serves as a point of departure for their systems of classification; though it is not usually formulated among the more primitive, it is clearly similar to the Chinese Taoist cosmogony, founded on the principle of male and female, without the union of which no universal harmony can exist.

The role of women in Toma society can be defined in terms of this dual structure. Polygamy and a patriarchical regime seem at first glance to confirm male superiority. It is the male who transmits the name of his clan, the *nien,* to his children. Jealous of his prerogatives, he tries constantly to assert his authority; but I concluded that all in all his authority was rather limited. The woman's situation is by no means as miserable as a hasty observation might indicate. A simple examination of the division of labor is proof: the male Toma must clear the *lugan,* till the soil, build the hut, weave cloth, collect firewood, while the women sow, weed, cook, spin, and fetch water. Remembering that each man has at least four wives, we must admit that a certain balance of forces is maintained.

Then, too, the women do not live cloistered like Moslem women; they circulate freely from one village to another, participate in festivities, and can be divorced simply by persuading their parents, or the prospective second husband, to reimburse the marriage portion of the scorned husband.

And if the men terrorize them with witchcraft, the women defend themselves by a more subtle magic and send equally fearful spirits against them. Voiné told us that among the Toma of Liberia women were in command at least in religious affairs. That case is neither isolated nor surprising. Practically all over the world, women have long been reputed to possess greater magic powers. Many more fairies and witches live in Europe's popular traditions than sorcerers or wizards. And in all the villages of the Toma country we noticed that old women held incontestable authority. During this celebration now taking place, for example, the prestige of the enormous woman witch-doctor could outweigh that of even the district chief.*

A movement in the shadow pulled me out of these reflections.

* See Appendix, IX: "Why Men Must Not Trust Women."

CHAPTER NINE

171

Voiné had come to sit beside me. There was a question on the tip of my tongue, but I hesitated a bit; I had no wish to outrage his beliefs.

"Don't you think that the old women know the men's secrets, that they know how you make the Afwi speak?"

In the half-darkness I sensed his smile.

"Of course. Those who have been initiated know . . . but they've never seen it."

I hadn't expected so blunt a confession, but another of Voiné's comments came to mind: "If the Toma had airplanes, a secret as strong as that, they'd hide them deep in the bush where no one could see them, and they'd sacrifice bulls and toss kola nuts over them."

Once more I had fallen on that same sense of theater, a love of the occult for its own sake, of secrecy for the sake of secrecy.

───────

My head heavy, I woke up in low spirits. Beside me, Jean crawled lazily out of his hammock. We had hardly closed our eyes. The gasping of tireless maracas had gone on uninterrupted the whole night through.

The door opened. Zézé slouched in, hunched forward, his face swollen, his eyes lifeless. In fear or fever, he trembled. Voiné followed him with a dismal, sunken expression.

"They've set spells on him," he said, gesturing at Zézé. "They've bewitched him."

Zézé groped for the tail of his old patched tunic, raised it, and showed us an enormous abscess at the anus. He was sure he had been poisoned by his enemies.

"It's nothing," I said, a little impressed in spite of myself. "We'll fix it up in no time."

"No." Voiné was stubborn. "It's voodoo. We can't fight it."

Disregarding that opinion, Jean administered two aureomycin tablets, and advised Zézé to get back to bed. He would wake him for subsequent treatments.

The square was calm again in early sunlight. Three or four old men, squatting against a hut, were still shaking maracas. The exhausted dancers were asleep. Men naked under their draped blankets strolled among the huts. As they chatted they brushed their teeth with white fibrous twigs. Bluish smoke, thickened by the humidity, rose into the clear air from thatched roofs saturated with rain water. Women were preparing wood fires.

Back in our room, we were having a small cup of wine. The door opened silently. The sacrifice-wife slipped into the room, her pale face expressionless. She stepped forward, held out her hand, took a cup. I filled it. She drank it off, murmured in a voice without timbre: *"Mamayo . . ."* and left.

It was the first and last time that we would hear her voice.

That afternoon the tom-tom orchestra of Orapossu made its entry into the village. The crowd streamed out in front of the five men, who were advancing toward Koli's hut to the rhythm of their shoulder-slung drums. The women surrounded them, protesting, gesturing wildly. The maraca orchestra stopped playing; the old women debated heatedly, with furious faces. These were days reserved for the women's celebration. What did these intruders want?

On the doorsill beside Koli, who was nodding with satisfaction, we listened to the tom-toms. The rhythms would have been the envy of the best jazz drummers.

Voiné was overjoyed. "There isn't another tom-tom that speaks so well in the whole Toma country."

But the women were still furious.

Koli, magnanimous, signaled to the musicians; they stopped, and he announced that they would play in the evening. He sent them off to quarters in a hut; the huts were already bursting with all the Toma invited to the festivities.

We had hung a lamp on a pole in front of the hut. A whirlwind of nocturnal insects haloed it. Koli was presiding, in his folding chair. The spectators were massed in a semicircle.

In the hut, Jean switched on the tape recorder.

The five musicians danced in place or whirled to the rhythm of their drums. One after another, men detached themselves from the crowd, performed their own dances, and then gave bills, wreaths of *guinzé*, or bottles of wine to the musicians.

Voiné, who was holding the microphone and looking important, called orders and advice to the orchestra. But he couldn't resist the desire to dance in his turn; he handed the microphone to Tony and tripped a few circles in a stiffly prim, dignified step. In the audience teeth shone very white under the harsh light of the lamp.

Zézé must have been in great pain, lying in a hammock beneath the hut's awning.

"You have to dance," Voiné said, back at the microphone. "They want to see how you dance."

Each of us gave a short demonstration and made a gift to the musicians.

Startling and close, just against the wall of the hut, the maracas attacked. The women had had enough of this competition. For a moment there was a sharp battle between the frantic rattle of maracas and the percussion of the tom-toms. But it was the women's celebration. The tom-toms yielded; the circle of spectators broke up and the old women's chorus rose again in the night.

The celebration had already lasted four days. We knew by heart the pantomimes of the hunt, of clearing the brush, of cooking, of war. . . . It had become impossible to walk through the village without falling into a trap set by the excised women, greedy for gifts.

Now we were worried about Zézé—he was still aflame with fever—and we could no longer enjoy the dances. With nothing special in mind, we wandered around the village. Koli, sitting on a tomb, was smoking a cigarette and gossiping with one of his innumerable children.

"You know all about motors," he said. "Maybe you could repair mine."

Jean and Tony needed no further urging. With the same enthusiasm they plunged under the hood of the Matford. My aversion to mechanics was such that I preferred to go on strolling around the huts.

We had filmed, recorded, and photographed all phases of the initiates' return; but some incident might occur, an unexpected scene that would be worth shooting.

"If you need us, we can be ready in a couple of minutes," Jean said. "We've been standing around with cameras at the ready for three months now. A little distraction won't hurt."

I walked in circles, watched the dancers from a distance, went to see Zézé several times—he was slowly recovering—and at the end of the day, exhausted by inaction, I too dove into the motor, up to the elbows in grease. A wasted effort. Two hours before, Tony and Jean had discovered that the chassis was cracked and that all the insulators had been devoured by termites.

Zézé reappeared at supper, somewhat relaxed. He showed us the abscess, open and healing well.

"*Merci*," he said, using French for the first time.

That evening we were doing more recordings of the tom-tom orchestra, and in the middle of the job the motor cut out. This time nothing could be done about it; the spark-plug was gone for good. We'd have to fetch another from Macenta. Tony, an indefatigable hiker, volunteered for the job immediately.

A mob of dignitaries, women, and children had jammed into the hut around the machines. Koli ordered his phonograph and records set up on the long table, and settled back in his armchair. One of his boys was assigned to the crank. In a churchly silence, the needle was lowered and the squeaking began. The phonograph was as fascinating to the children as our tape recorder.

Successively, we heard *valses musettes*, Lucienne Boyer, South American music, Bach, Laverne, and very old recordings by Yvette Guilbert.

We had just turned in when Voiné entered the room with a beaming smile. "A witch-doctor has died in Kovobakoro, close by. We ought to go over. There isn't a woman left in the village. All the male secrets will be brought out in honor of the witch-doctor, and you'll be able to film them."

This was an unhoped-for chance. First thing in the morning we asked Koli's permission; the ceremony would take place in his district. He had no objections. He put twenty bearers at our disposal and promised to meet us in Kovobakoro, where he would make whatever arrangements were necessary.

It was our last day in Bueylazu. We spent it chatting with Koli, strolling around the village, packing our equipment, and watching the excised women's dances, which ended at twilight.

After the evening meal we returned to our room. The maraca orchestra was playing right outside, and we had to scream at each other.

"It's getting to be a little too much!" Jean shouted, stretching out in his hammock.

We touched on the next day's ceremony.

"You can give odds that it won't go off without a hitch," Tony called from his small bed in the corner of the room.

CHAPTER NINE

177

We were all pretty sure of that. The difficulties would not suddenly disappear now. That would have been too easy.

Under the awning in an adjacent nook separated from us by a partition with a small opening, Zézé and Wego, in their hammocks, had kept their lantern lit, as always. The door between us and the larger room was open. We heard Voiné come in. He wasn't alone. In the shadows we made out a buxom figure. Taking advantage of the general euphoria, Voiné had temporarily appropriated one of the district chief's two-hundred-odd wives. He came to the doorway, greeted us with a gesture, and closed the door discreetly.

Jean, run down by the work of the previous few days, had fallen asleep. The rattle of maracas diminished steadily. One by one the old women were returning to their huts.

"It's unbelievable," Tony said. "I can almost hear my own voice."

I dimmed the lantern, pushed it close to the wall at the foot of the bed, and stretched out beside Jean. The rattle of maracas had died. A murmuring, palpable silence fell upon the village.

I closed my eyes.

Suddenly, right at the wall of the hut, rose a three-note melody on the flute. The midnight flute of Macenta. An instant later it was in the large room where Voiné slept. Then it skipped up to the roof, just overhead. I sat up on my bed. Jean slept on.

At the first sounds, Zézé and Wego had extinguished their lantern. I heard them murmuring together.

"This time they're going a little too far," said Tony, who had come to sit beside me.

The light tinkling of a bell joined the flute song, and the music began to drift around the hut, through the walls. I dimmed the lamp.

"What are we going to do?" Tony said.

"Let's wait a little while."

"Let's try to grab hold of one, if we can."

The door facing the square was open. We stepped to it on tiptoe. Outside, a full moon bathed the village in pale light and threw the circular huts into relief. Nothing moved.

The music went on. It came from everywhere and nowhere.

"*Formidable,*" Tony murmured.

A shower of pebbles rained suddenly on the iron roof. Then another, echoing like a drum roll. The pebbles scraped along the corrugations and fell to the gravel at our feet.

We went back inside and sat on the bed, struck dumb.

Two or three more volleys of pebbles crackled against the roof. Zézé and Wego were still murmuring. The flute zigzagged in all directions. A frantic sound of galloping passed in front of the hut. We jumped to the doorway. The village was absolutely still in the moonlight.

"It's a little strong," Tony said.

In front of us the earth resounded once more. I squinted. A herd of maddened goats bolted by near the hut; and yet I saw nothing. Not the slightest movement. In the distance rose the Afwi's voice.

Stupidly, we stood rooted.

"They're giving us both barrels!"

Jean was still asleep.

Toward three in the morning the full moon set behind the trees. The flute song trailed off; the Afwi's voice was still. A heavy silence enveloped the village again. Voiné, in the next room, sighed a deep sigh. Zézé and Wego lit their lantern and exchanged a few words in normal voices.

In the morning we questioned all three of them. They had seen nothing, heard nothing, felt nothing.

Now we knew that our initiation had not solved the problem at all.

TEN

The musicians from Orapossu came along with Jean and me. Tony, though sorely tired by our nocturnal adventure, had left for Macenta on Koli's bicycle at dawn, under a gray sky. He would meet us to-night in Kovobakoro.

Koli had a little unfinished business to straighten out, but he would go on horseback and would join us later with the bearers and equipment.

Everything was working out smoothly.

Voiné was unusually talkative this morning. Zézé's rapid cure had given him confidence, and he promised to see to it that we attended all the burial ceremonies. On the way to Kovobakoro he described the different rituals we would film. It was true that not a woman remained in the village. They had all retreated far into the bush: the great secret mask was to come out in broad daylight and march through every street of the village, escorted by the Afwi's sacred music. Then all parts of the corpse with any magical value would be cut away and used in the preparation of medicines: the skin of the forehead, the liver, the left hand. The skin of the forehead symbolized intelligence; the liver, a vital organ, physical strength; and the left hand, the hand that held the trident, occult power. Then the corpse would be rolled in thorns placed within the mat that covered it.

"The witch-doctor made many people suffer greatly while he was alive," Voiné explained. "Now they take revenge."

If the dead man's family were rich, it could buy up the parts of the body cut away, and the witch-doctor's powers would remain among them. Otherwise there would be a division among the witch-doctors present.

The Afwi accompanied the corpse right to the grave, and when the pit was filled the whole village participated in the usual sacrifices.

Dark clouds were rolling across a dull sky. In half an hour at the outside we would be in Kovobakoro. The musicans preceding us stopped at a trail-crossing; then the tom-toms surrounded us, and their energy redoubled.

"They won't go any farther," Voiné said. "They can't go in there where a dead man is."

Voiné performed a last little dance within the orchestra's circle. We distributed farewell gifts to the musicians and left them there.

The village lay on two levels of sand and black rock. When we arrived it seemed paralyzed. No voice. No pestle driving against a mortar. No woman before her hut.

Groups of squatting men chatted in quiet voices and hardly turned to welcome us. A little put out, we sat down in front of a hut. Voiné looked around with a worried expression. In a few moments the village chief appeared. Reluctant, shifty-eyed, he twisted his turban in nervous fingers and bobbed his head in an attitude of feigned submission. He apologized for being late, declared himself highly honored by our visit, and offered us a very small empty hut, hardly large enough for Jean and me. Then he disappeared. His hospitality ended there. He sent us none of the usual gifts.

"Enter the villain, twirling mustaches," Jean said.

It didn't matter. A few hours from now Koli would set everything right.

At the time of day when Toma men worked their *lugans*, the men of Kovobakoro were lazing around the village. But aside from that fact, nothing indicated that an important death had just occurred. We had not yet seen the dead man's hut or heard the traditional lamentations. Our equipment was arriving at wide intervals, bit by bit, but the essential material, particularly the indispensable generator, was still missing. A bearer gleaming with sweat deposited a crate of unexposed film at our feet. Through Voiné, we questioned him. According to him, Koli was winding up his preparations for departure. We waited a few hours more. All the bearers, coming in one after another, brought us the same news: Koli was saddling up and on his way.

We walked around the village without gleaning a single friendly glance. Slowly, in small groups, the women returned from the bush; they set to winnowing, or to pounding rice in front of their huts.

"Look," Jean said. "A white woman!"

We had seen her at the same moment. She was a tall, thin woman, pounding rice with long elastic movements. She was so fair-skinned that at first she seemed much more nude than the others.

Several of the villagers, in fact, looked amazingly European, as much by their color as by their features. One of the men, seated in front of the nearest hut, who was watching us with a wary eye and smoking his pipe, was the picture of a career sergeant.

I said so to Voiné. He smiled. "You know," he said, "this was old Kowo's district, the chief who wanted to fight the whites. But they hauled cannon up on the mountain there." He pointed to a verdant promontory that dominated the forest. "They fired. The warriors had never seen that. They ran away. Kowo too—but he's buried here just the same."

He led us outside the village. A tombstone stood on a butte, at the foot of a huge dead tree.

"It's up there," he said. "Kowo should have listened to old Kréan, who made peace with the whites right away, but Kowo was a great chief. He never had a sword or a rifle or even a stick. When he spoke, everybody trembled. He was as tall as the Laniboi, and at night he flew over the huts. He was the last of the tall men."

"What were the men like, before Kowo?"

"They were all as tall as the huts."

"You mean the Toma?"

"No," Voiné said. "All men were like that. The Toma didn't exist."

"But how did they come to be?"

"They came together from everywhere. Old Zézé, his grand-fathers came from the savanna. . . . Now they're all pure Toma."

In general, tombs were within the village limits. I was surprised to see old Kowo's so far out.

"Kowo Bakoro was much bigger," Voiné explained. "There was even another village close by, but all the people left it."

Beyond the tomb we climbed a narrow trail. In the middle of a wide cleared space on top of the hill there was a small, isolated, round hut, almost intact; all around it were circles of tamped earth, surrounded here and there by slabs of wall. The thick vegetation had not yet reconquered this plateau; only a sparse grass grew. A breach in the wall of great trees gave us a glimpse of the dark green mass of forest below; its rolling hills ran off like long swells to the misty horizon. Voiné pointed. "Over there is Soguru," he said, as if he had guessed my obsession.

We retraced our steps. Voiné showed us a rocky, moss-covered dirt road dipping sharply downhill through the bush. Networks of liana barred approach. The road was never used and was not kept up. I stepped out on it, attracted by the mysterious aspect of the place.

"If you want," Voiné said. "But that's where the ancestors are worshipped, and I have no right to lead you through it."

This sudden evasion on the part of a usually brash Voiné intrigued me. The abrupt, slippery trail dropped between tall blocks of black rock. Draperies of moss trailed to the ground from the boulders and the liana. In the humid green shade I felt as though in a Jules Verne landscape. On a wide flat rock at the roadside, offerings had been heaped up. I stopped for a moment, went on downhill, and suddenly found myself on the outskirts of the village.

That was why Voiné had not wanted to guide us too ostentatiously. He was afraid the whole village would rise up against him. After that incident, Koli's backing was more than ever indispensable. But night fell, and he had given no sign.

Old Zézé was waiting in the hut with some bad news for us. The elders had ordered him to inform us that the dead man had not been a very great witch-doctor, and that his funeral would not be the occasion for any special rites.

CHAPTER TEN

185

"But they're lying," Voiné added, "and old Zézé didn't want to force their hand. We'll have to wait for Koli. If he gives the order, you'll be able to see everything."

All the women were back in the village now. And from a neighboring hut rose keening for the dead.

The two witch-doctors, Jean, and I were sitting in the darkness of our hut, silent. For the moment, we had no reason to worry. Tony hadn't arrived yet with the spare parts. But in his own corner Zézé chewed the cud of bitterness. For the first time witch-doctors formerly under his authority had defied him successfully.

———

The generator finally came along the next morning. Jean and I got to work setting it up. Most of the villagers took no interest in these preparations. We were under strict quarantine. Only a few of the more curious boys watched the trial runs. According to the last bearers, Koli, held up yesterday by an urgent problem, would surely join us today.

Jean was unrolling wire from the generator to the hut when a sudden stampede broke out in the village. The natives dove for their huts. Into the deserted square galloped a bull; he roared to a stop and snorted, his nostrils bloody. In the doorway of the hut where we had taken shelter, Voiné explained that the animal had broken his hobble during a sacrifice in Bueylazu and had escaped after being wounded by a shot.

Several men stepped out of a hut with a gourd full of salt. They took careful steps toward the bull. He pawed the ground, thrust his head forward as if to charge, and then wheeled suddenly and disappeared in the bush. No one even tried to chase after him.

Nothing indicated that a ceremony would take place. We finished setting up the equipment anyway. Men were palavering within the huts; the hammering of pestles echoed through the village. We were all ready to shoot. Annoyed at the cold shoulder we had been given, we kept to our hut, relaxing in the hammocks.

Toward noon the elders decided to pay us a visit. They seemed a little less hostile. According to them, the man who was to be buried had not been a witch-doctor, but only the master hunter; if we wished, we could film the ceremonies in his honor. After last night's discussion it was clear that this was a compromise maneuver, intended to give us partial satisfaction.

"It's not true," Voiné whispered furiously. "Don't even take your machines outside."

I was inclined to agree with him, but didn't want to ignite a hot discussion that might turn the witch-doctors against us again. I preferred to wait for a solution (without really believing in it) in Koli's arrival. We followed the elders to the dead man's hut.

All the hunters had assembled in the square in their bush outfits: monkey-skin toques and filthy, colorless, ragged tunics. Decked with small sacks of powder and hunting charms, they had their rifles cocked. Some thirty yellowish dogs dozed at their feet. I would not have believed that so small a village could muster so large a pack. One by one the men entered the hut. The corpse was there, rolled in a reed mat on the bare ground. A hunter touched the mat and ordered all his dogs to lie on it. When each hunter had completed this rite, they all assembled around a tomb, and debated the division of the dead man's hunting lands.

I passed the time playing with one of the hunting dogs who

seemed affectionate. One of the elders snickered when he saw me, turned to the others, and said a few words; they all laughed. Voiné translated the comment bitterly: "The old man says you've chosen the worst of all the dogs—the one who's never learned to hunt."

I had forgotten that the Koiwogui were not only warriors and chiefs, but also hunters. Voiné, in high repute as a hunter throughout the region, found it intolerable that his *patron* couldn't distinguish between good and bad dogs at first glance.

"If you had a rifle," he added regretfully, "I could go with them and tonight I'd bring back a black doe. They'll certainly find game. The dead man gave them all his power, and the dogs will find tracks."

The hunters separated and disappeared rapidly into the bush.

To our great astonishment, four men returned to the hut and brought out the corpse. We followed them to a freshly dug pit that we had not previously noticed. With no ceremony, they dropped the corpse into the hole and started to shovel earth over it. We hardly knew what to think. Zézé and Voiné, outraged, watched this unexpected move in silence. We withdrew to our hut, much disappointed. Even if Koli came now, it would be too late.

"They have no right to do that," Voiné protested. "The spirit of the dead man will take revenge. He won't let them sleep."

Following Zézé, he went to join the elders in the village chief's hut. We expected nothing to come of this discussion. We thought we might as well not have set up our equipment.

Night fell. Our two witch-doctors, obviously shocked, crossed the square and signaled us to join them. After closing the door of the hut they spoke first between themselves in low voices. Then Voiné turned to us.

"The old man knows very well what's going to happen. Now Koli won't come at all. . . ."

He gave us the inside story. Koli had simply asked the villagers to permit us to film; he had not given orders. The villagers had refused. Zézé had told them that we knew all the secrets already and that there was nothing to fear.

"Maybe you're not afraid to die," they told him; "you can show the whites whatever you want to, but we won't have any part of it."

Informed of their decision, Koli Zumanigui had not insisted and, on the pretext of urgent business, had gone off to let the affair settle itself.

"They buried the man just like that," Voiné said. "When you're gone, they'll dig him up for the ceremonies."

We hadn't foreseen any such duplicity. So in spite of all Zézé's authority, even in spite of his example, the witch-doctors would sooner run the risk of the dead man's fury than reveal to us secrets that we already knew. I turned to Zézé, who was lying back in the shadows.

"You haven't been able to do anything here," I told him. "In this little village they refuse to obey you, even to let us film a burial. Do you think you can do more at Soguru? Give orders to the three thousand Toma who'll be there?"

The old master witch-doctor stood up. He spoke in a strong voice, and Voiné translated with all his old assurance: "All that you say is true. Here, Koli commands. I did not wish to give orders myself. As for Soguru, I'll get there first, before you, and nothing will stop me. I am the master of the tattooing, the strongest. To succeed, Voiné and I will pass through the fire. The Guelemlai have not yet come, and there is time."

He left without another word.

We knew nothing about the rite he had just alluded to, but we knew that the Toma considered fire the greatest of all natural forces. They kept fires going all night in their huts, and, Voiné told us: "When a man doesn't eat enough meat, when he has no strength left, he has to sit beside the fire for a long time. It replaces meat." In very grave circumstances—for example, when a witch-doctor wanted to dominate a rival—he retired to the sacred wood and with the help of his assistants constructed a kind of gridded basket of green wood to be hung three or four feet above a hearth; he sat in it with all his charms and remained there invoking the spirits. The rite had to be repeated over seven consecutive days, and had to be accompanied by absolute sexual continence.

Now Voiné seemed in a hurry to get back to Tuwelu. It was his opinion that it would be useless to wait for Tony, who would catch up to us later.

"These villagers are hard-headed," he said. "They'll wait forever, but they won't do a thing in front of us."

Regretfully, we decided to take his advice; we set our departure for the next morning. Once more we packed our equipment. Jean was discouraged. We had nothing to say to each other.

ELEVEN

The problem of bearers, at least, was nonexistent this morning. The inhabitants of Kovobakoro were so eager to see us leave that every able-bodied man in the community volunteered to help us. Our equipment went before. It was our first trip under just these circumstances; and to avoid mishaps, involuntary or not, Jean, Voiné, and I ranged continually up and down the column.

A series of storms had transformed the dry earth of the trails into shiny, thick puddled clay. Sharp dips and steep hills followed one after another and made traveling worse. The red ants, rarely seen during the dry season, were abundant now with the rains. They crossed the trail in spotty triangles that might spread across three or four yards. And the bearers had to hop rapidly across the endless swarming streams of them, two or three inches deep, to avoid being bitten by the "warriors." The Toma's agility over these bad stretches, with a sixty-five-pound crate on his head, was incredible. And the four men carrying the particularly unwieldy generator were no less skillful than the others.

A river barred the route. A cable of twined branches crossed it, supported by oscillating forks buried in the mud. The river was about thirty feet wide. Very erect, the bearers crossed, not hesitating under their loads; even the generator, balanced on the heads of two of the stockiest, crossed with no difficulty. From the far bank the Toma, taking a breather, watched us. We must have been ludicrous

THE SACRED FOREST

in our tightrope-walker's poses, arms outstretched, bodies swaying, toes curled tight against the slippery wood.

Two short but violent storms overtook us in the heart of the bush, between the numerous villages along the trail. Everywhere the warm welcome given us contrasted with that of Kovobakoro; we had to stop often en route to greet various dignitaries.

Only one village separated us from Tuwelu; we were hurrying to arrive before a coming storm. Behind, a cry stopped us: it was a young boy bringing us a chicken. He explained to Voiné that we had not stopped long enough in the last village, and that an elder had ordered the gift sent after us.

"That's an uncle of the one you took care of," Voiné said. "The one who's always falling off palm trees. The old man is very angry that you didn't wait. He came back from his *lugan* to see you. He sends you this chicken and wants you to come back another time."

At Tuwelu we felt at home. The natives greeted us with displays of friendship truly touching after our experience of the previous few days. We moved back into our hut, re-creating the familiar chaos immediately, as maniacally as old bachelors. The day went by in moving things around and checking over the equipment. We waited impatiently for Tony, but at nightfall he had not yet arrived.

To our surprise, he showed up on foot at eleven at night, covered with mud and scratches. He had left the bicycle in Bofosso. Voiné and Zézé couldn't believe their eyes. They would never have admitted that a white man could move at night, with no lantern, alone in the deep bush. They rose immediately, wrapped in their blankets, and brought him kola nuts and palm wine in token of their admiration; they ordered water heated so that he could bathe. The news spread through the village rapidly. Elders, old women, children, filed through the hut to contemplate this phenomenon: a white man who trekked at night like a witch-doctor. Even before eating and drinking, Tony reported to us on his trip.

"We're in bad shape," he said in a low voice. "We'll talk about it later." Then, in a normal tone: "I absolutely had to get back tonight. It seems that the celebration at Soguru will be held very soon. I wanted to warn you. I thought I'd be here before nightfall, but what with all the rivers and mud and rain, I was held up. In the low savanna between Serissu and here, my heart was really in my mouth. I had the feeling an animal was following me. I lit matches and kept cigarettes going, thinking that fire might scare him off."

"There's a lot of panthers in that savanna," Voiné remarked.

"I know. I spent most of my time losing the trail. You can get along at night in the woods, but in the savanna— Anyway, I could feel the trail better barefoot. When I got back into the bush, about fifteen minutes from Tuwelu, I felt a hot breath right up against me. I jumped about twelve feet straight up. When I came down again I lit a match. It was a bull. Then I knew I was almost here."

"But that was the mad bull from Kovobakoro," Voiné said.

Tony reacted with an energetic and heartfelt oath.

"At night all the animals are rounded up now, because of the rice," Voiné went on. The seedlings were about to break through the earth now, and for several days the village had been belted by a solid corral: lianas strung from tree to tree in the bush.

When we were alone in the hut, Tony got to the bad news. "They

CHAPTER ELEVEN

193

all know now that we've been tattooed and seen secrets. The district commander is pretty upset. He says that the witch-doctors will do anything to see us properly punished, even poison us or stir up the populace against us. He wants to avoid trouble, and he's thinking of canceling our authorization, to stop the photography. We have no time to lose."

After a quick discussion, we decided to move on to Soguru as soon as possible, to do the groundwork and learn the exact date of the ceremonies.

———

The next morning in the crisp dawn a long line of patients was already waiting at our door. They wanted to be treated before leaving for their *lugans*. Men sharpened their machetes in long precise strokes against the standing tombstones. The natives of Tuwelu now trusted us so completely that they did not hesitate to bring us their children, who accepted treatment and even injections with perfect stoicism.

When clinic hours were over, Zézé and Voiné came along. "You'll have to visit Zézé's wives' hut," Voiné said to Jean, the resident practitioner. "One of his wives gave birth last night, and the baby is dead. You'll have to treat the woman."

Zézé and Voiné were impassive. In their eyes this death was not even remotely an evil omen. Nor was it a punishment: the child was simply not fated to live.

Without transition, Voiné added in the same indifferent voice: "You can get your machines ready. The Guelemlai are coming today."

This was the first harbinger of the great tattooing. In a few days we would know where we stood.

"Well, it won't be long now," Jean said gloomily.

Tony and I had nothing to add to that remark. A tacit understanding grew among us: there was no use even talking about the slight chance we had of filming the ceremonies. We were sitting in our hammocks, worried. Voiné had stepped out of the hut.

Suddenly he reappeared, excited. "The Guelemlai!" he shouted. "The Guelemlai are here!"

All the Bilakoro were assembled in one corner of the square, squeezed back against a hut, behind a tomb, like a panicked herd. For the occasion they were wearing a kind of Phrygian helmet of panther-skin with a goatskin fringe, encrusted with cowrie shells, and dalmatics made up of varicolored patches of hide; these were vestiges of the old warrior caste.

A few puddles still glistened in the sunlight. Those village boys who were already tattooed stood between the huts, their arms ringed with bracelets and their lips limed, with long branches barring the way to the whitened forest messengers. The Guelemlai, their features frozen under the pallid make-up, moved through a slow-motion ballet, trying symbolically to force a passage with their white poles. No chants, no music. Only the children's cries troubled the silence, and the scraping of poles on the gravel, and the rustling of the long raffia fringes.

The master of the Guelemlai, wearing long trousers under his tunic and a cowboy hat, stepped out before the natives assembled in the square. He paced back and forth, brandishing a switch of dried herbs, and demanded offerings. Each of the men of Tuwelu made his contribution to the great ceremony, after the usual short oration. Indifferent to these transactions, the Guelemlai continued to whirl about the village in their heavy horse-collars. They were trying to reach the Bilakoro without coming into range of our cameras. From the beginning they had resisted all attempts at photography; they dodged away when we edged toward them. Little boys of six or seven, not yet ready for initiation, uttered yelps of joy and watched us with delighted smiles: the Guelemlai, of whom they were so afraid, were in turn terrified by us.

The ceremony took up a major part of the afternoon. Then suddenly the protective barrier yielded; the Bilakoro fled in a body toward the forest, followed by the whitened men—and this time Jean succeeded in filming them in flight.

Back in the village the smaller children gathered around our hut, laughing and chattering. Their young voices chorused repeatedly a word we did not understand. I asked Voiné: "What are they saying?"

"Guelemlai-hunters. They call you that because you made the Guelemlai afraid."

The children crowded into the hut, but Zézé came in after them and sent them flying with a brief gesture. He wanted to speak to us alone.

His advice only confirmed what we had felt the evening before. We should go to see the district chief of the Ulamai, responsible for the great tattooing of that group, to win his support. This chief, very young, owed his nomination to the whites, and it was Zézé's opinion that he could not refuse us. Voiné would guide us to him. Zézé, already over-compromised, would remain in Tuwelu to be "heated" by Wego. We would leave in the morning.

———

After a hard march we reached the district chief's village. A few women were working in front of their huts. Finally a man appeared; he offered to guide us to a near-by hamlet where, it seemed, the district chief could be found. We went back along the trail and then cut off to a new path. The district chief, informed of our arrival, came out to meet us. He was a skinny young man with a nervous, sickly appearance. His welcome sounded hypocritical and theatrical. He carried a huge cane and wore a Basque beret pulled down over his head like a skullcap. We all went back to his village, and he received us formally in his hut.

The hut's interior was a curious compromise between classic Toma and *salle à manger Henri II*. Everywhere little red flounces decorated rough-hewn furniture, the work of local artisans. Photographs of forgotton movie stars hung side by side with those of fallen politicians. Lebrun stared out from an immense frame. The chief sat down behind a wide desk covered with a flowered cloth. We seated ourselves across from him. Like all district chiefs, he spoke French fluently. But contrary to all expectations, he made no effort to inform himself of the purpose of our visit; he was generous, though, with gratuitous expressions of friendship. We brought out the classic gift: a bottle of rum. With a troubled, bilious eye he stammered vague thanks and tucked the bottle away in a desk drawer. I had never before seen a Toma behave that way. Alcohol was drunk, it was not cached away for a rainy day: this was part of the tribal temperament.

Having exposed the treasures of his hut for our admiration (various household articles, postcards, magazines), he interrupted the conversation brusquely—it had touched on tattooing—saying that he must see to a meal and quarters for us.

"There is a great charlatan here," Voiné said as we stepped out into the square. "I want to see him."

Then we entered a shadowy hut already occupied by several old men. They greeted us amicably and squeezed together to make room for us. A relative intimacy sprang up. I discovered then how well assimilated we were. The Toma accepted us without reservations, went to no particular trouble for us; and yet by a curious contradiction they refused to admit us to their secret rites.

The charlatan, in a filthy tunic, unrolled a mat full of sand and smoothed the sand in front of us. His eyes half-closed, he began to trace cabalistic signs with mechanical gestures; the signs were much like those of the North African geomancers. For half an hour, silent, he let his fingers wander across the sand. When there remained no room for writing, he erased everything with a sweeping gesture and began again.

Finally, slowly, he spoke; Voiné listened, his wide eyes on the charlatan's face. He was as fascinated now as he had been when Virel read his fortune in the tarots. He turned to us.

"I have to make a gift to the women of my family and kill a white cock on my father's tomb. After that everything will go smoothly, and I may become district chief."

I had thought fleetingly of requesting a consultation for myself. But I was disappointed in this oracle. I had expected far more interesting revelations.

The thin figure of the district chief appeared in the doorway. "Dinner's ready," he said simply.

We followed him into an impeccably tidy hut. In the middle of the floor a large bowl of rice and the traditional chicken cooked in palm oil awaited us. We had brought no utensils; we squatted and ate in the Toma manner.

Voiné disappeared with the district chief. A few moments later he came back and sat down again. He seemed pleased.

"The little chief will help us," he said. "He'll talk to the elders for us."

We found it difficult to share his optimism. We had had time to exchange impressions of our host. He hardly inspired us with confidence.

In any case he came to take his leave a few moments later, with an absent air: an urgent affair called him to a near-by village.

We left when he did. On the way back we all followed the same trail for a time. In the distance, above the green waves of the forest, we saw the abrupt bluff of Oko, which dominates Tuwelu. We reached a flat covered with black boulders, where our paths diverged.

This time we would not pass up the chance of a clear and direct answer, but the little chief managed to wiggle away again.

CHAPTER ELEVEN

"There is always a hut ready for you in my village," he said. "I don't know when the tattooing will be and I haven't the power to permit you to film it. I'll have to speak to the elders. I'll tell you afterward."

He gave us no time to insist; he was off into the bush, his cane in hand.

Voiné was gasping with indignation. "The little chief was lying. In a week all the witch-doctors will be in his village for the ceremonies, and he knows it, and if he wants to, he can give orders to the elders."

The sky was heavy, an unbroken expanse of gray. In front of our hut in Tuwelu we were treating the last of the morning's patients. A man arrived and handed me a confidential letter bearing the Macenta district seal. Nervously I ripped open the envelope. Tony and Jean read over my shoulder. The district commander requested my presence urgently. The letter said nothing more. Voiné watched our anxious faces attentively.

"Bad news?" he asked.

"No, it's nothing. The district commander wants to see us."

He relaxed immediately: among white men, problems were rapidly smoothed away.

We gathered in the hut to talk it over. It was surely bad news, as Voiné had guessed. The district commander wanted to inform me personally of his decision to interrupt our work. There was no room for doubt. We decided that I would leave right away and plead for a reprieve. In my absence Tony and Jean would film the transition and background scenes that the cutters would need later, and would record all they could in Tuwelu.

In spite of the humid heat and the onset of a fever, I was so worried that I never noticed the length of the trip. Barefoot, I hiked rapidly down the trail. Because I was going to the big town, I carried "truck-skin" sandals: Greek sandals cut out of old tires. The Diulas sold them in the market.

I hardly looked around as I marched. How could I fix things in Macenta? Suddenly my right foot plunged into a swarming magma. I jumped. Too late. I had stepped smack into a column of ants. My leg was covered with them halfway up the calf. I squashed them, chased them wildly, but the warriors' jaws were buried deep into my flesh. A painful burning streaked through my thigh. The main thing was not to stop moving. I was limping when I reached Bofosso. My leg was half-paralyzed, stiff from ankle to hip.

Luckily it was Thursday, market day, and I very soon found a truck to take me into Macenta. It was a miserable trip. Shooting pains throbbed in my side.

I hardly recognized Macenta. The whole village seemed asleep under the leaden sky. Whatever else happened, I would pick up the mail. I went to the post office. The clerks were sitting out front, smoking and playing *belote*. My surprise was obvious.

"Nobody works on Ascension Day," one of them told me.

We had lived outside the calendar for too long. I had lost any notion of holidays, fixed or movable.

I hesitated to appear before the district commander on a holiday and in my bush outfit: truck-skin sandals, old shorts, torn shirt, uncut hair flying wildly, beard scraggly; but I had to know his decision immediately, and I set off for his home. After all, my clothes were only of secondary importance.

That illusion did not last long. I crossed the bright-blooming formal garden, mounted the steps, and irrupted suddenly into an elegant cocktail party. My unexpected presence quite obviously dampened the proceedings. Considerably embarrassed, I tried to put a good face on it. The district commander, friendly and not at all surprised, drew me into a corner. He had no final decision to transmit to me. He was only afraid of reprisals the witch-doctors might make against us, and announced that he was tired of receiving complaints about us every day of the week. I defended our cause as well as I could, and told him once more that we accepted freely all risks that might attach to the work.

"I sent your dossier along to the governor," he said. "I can't stop your work until I've had an answer, but I advise you to finish up quickly."

Talking fast, I persuaded him to give us a two-week delay. I left the residency in a happy daze. Now we had more than enough time to film the tattooing: the ceremonies would take place within a week.

I wanted to go back immediately and tell Jean and Tony. But it was impossible to find a truck going back that day. I would spend the night in Macenta. I had forgotten my bites and my fever.

———

Tony and Jean were waiting impatiently.

"After you left," Jean said, "we shot all the backgrounds and transitions you wanted; but Voiné's in bad shape. He thinks he's been poisoned."

In the hut next to our own I found Voiné prostrate on the Toma bed, anguish in his eyes; he was buried to the chin in Tony's sleeping-bag. With a heavy effort he propped himself up on one elbow. "They poisoned me in Soguru," he said. "A good thing the *patrons* are taking care of me."

I tried to convince him that the fever, the vomiting, and the pain in his intestines were due to a simple attack of dysentery and not to the revenge of his enemies; but he refused to believe it.

"The conspiracy is on us, stronger than ever," he said. Then he added scornfully: "The little chief never even sent the note."

The district chief's answer should have arrived the day after our visit. My friends had heard nothing while I was gone.

Together in our hut, we held a council of war. Neither Jean nor Tony believed in the poison story. They had followed Voiné's illness for two days and were sure that it was a passing attack. Tomorrow he would be cured.

The news I had brought back forced us to act quickly. As the district chief had forgotten us, we would send him a messenger tomorrow; the messenger could nose around at the same time and give us a first-hand report on the witch-doctors' attitude. We needed a skilled and intelligent envoy for this mission. The chief bearer of Tuwelu had already rendered us great services. We went to find him. He knew a little French. He was a young boy with fine features and an open face, very taciturn. Without hesitation he agreed to be our spokesman.

The decision taken and the arrangements made, we felt less anxious. As we relaxed in our hammocks, old Voiné Beawogui put in his appearance. He had returned from one of his almost daily trips through the Toma country, and he told us bitterly that in several villages he had been barred from elders' meetings and refused entry to the sacred wood. All inhabitants of Tuwelu would henceforth be considered traitors.

The next day Voiné came to wake us a little later than usual. His face was drawn; he had been marked, as we had, by a sleepless night; yet he displayed an unexpected optimism. We told him about our most recent project. He approved, and immediately offered to go along with the head bearer.

"The *patrons* have cured me," he said. "I'm not afraid of anything now. I can go over there and explain things to the elders. They'll understand."

We made no effort to dissuade him. A few hours later the two men started off. We followed them to the village limits. I watched Voiné's long, loose-limbed figure disappear. In spite of his arrogance, his play-acting, and his crafty little tricks, he was a real friend to us. He would do anything to see us win out.

We had been waiting since the previous morning for the envoys' return. We had had time to imagine all possible solutions and to weigh our chances carefully. More and more we were doubtful of success. In a week the whole expedition might come to an end. These last days of impatience and uncertainty became a trial of nerve.

Before nightfall we decided to go out to meet the two messengers. We were hardly outside the village when we saw them coming up the trail. As soon as he saw us Voiné waved his black hat in sign of victory.

"The conspiracy is broken," he announced. "The elders have nothing against you. But they've sworn on the gri-gri not to show you anything. If you happen to come to Soguru just as the celebration begins, as if it was an accident, they won't be guilty, and you'll be able to shoot."

"That's right," the head bearer confirmed. "They can't invite you. They promised. But if you're there, they won't say anything."

That unexpected interpretation of ancestral law solved all our problems. The tattooing would take place the following Sunday, a week off; but preparations would begin, it seemed, on Thursday. We had no time to waste. We decided immediately to send our equipment ahead in crates, little by little. From village to village, by relays of bearers, it would arrive in Soguru without difficulty and we would catch up to it Thursday morning.

Unfortunately, most of the rites took place before dawn—and we had been waiting over a month for the indispensable magnesium flares. Once more Tony volunteered to go into Macenta to see if they came in Wednesday's mail.

We felt as though we had turned defeat to victory at the last moment. We did not know how to thank the two men who had carried the diplomatic negotiations to a successful end.

We spent the next day in enthusiastic preparations; we checked

CHAPTER ELEVEN

the crates, distributed the loads as evenly as possible, and watched them start, one by one, for Soguru.

Wednesday morning Voiné stepped into our hut and fell to the platform of tamped earth. He was the picture of dejection.

"The little chief sent your baggage back to the district limits. He forbids you to enter his territory."

This time we did not understand. It was true that with the passage of time we had become, to the Toma, beings somewhat apart, halfway between themselves and the *wigui*, but they had never treated us this way. In spite of the setback, we decided to follow our schedule. Tony left for Macenta, and we waited, suspending judgment, for confirmation of the bad, and to us unbelievable, news.

In the middle of the afternoon a messenger in a pith helmet appeared before us, snapping to attention; his bare feet stuck out below well-polished leggings. With terror in his eyes, he gave us a military salute. He was trembling from head to foot. He handed me a note from the district chief; it fluttered between his fingers. It was an indecipherable scribble; I asked him to explain it. He was too terrified to answer. Perhaps he was tired from the forced march he had made; we invited him to sit and offered him a cup of wine. His expression softened; slowly he regained confidence and managed to articulate a few words: the men of Soguru had told him that we would beat him, and possibly put him in irons, because he brought us very bad news. As Voiné had reported, the little chief, on orders of the witch-doctors, would oppose our arrival in his district, and by force if necessary.

We had not supposed that the sacrilege committed by our witch-doctor friends could engender consequences of such gravity. We knew the laws of Toma hospitality too well. No mistake, no confusion, was possible: that a chief should take this position was equivalent to a declaration of war.

During the conversation the natives of Tuwelu had entered the hut in great number. They took our part vociferously. An old woman whom we had treated brought us kola nuts in a token of friendship; most of the inhabitants followed suit soon after. The messenger was convinced.

"I'll tell them what I've seen," he said. "And they'll understand that you are the Toma's friends."

We asked him to transmit one last proposition: if we attended the tattooing, we would film only what the women were permitted to see.

With a final military salute, he left us, after assuring us that tomorrow morning at dawn, at the very latest, he would bring us a response himself.

────

We waited vainly for him; and on Voiné's instance we left for Soguru toward ten in the morning. The sky was very blue, the trail dry. We carried no baggage. Our purpose was to obtain one last interview with the district chief. Voiné himself made no attempt to disguise the risk attendant on our project.

We went through several villages, moving rapidly. The natives' attitude had changed in the previous few days. They came to greet us as we passed, but with reticence. Little by little Voiné lost his assurance; his steps slowed; he tried to joke, to draw the natives' sympathy; but his anxiety soon became anguish. He stopped us near a stream, went to gather long-stemmed reeds, and gave us each one.

"Take these," he said. "If you want to be strong at Soguru—there are many witch-doctors in Soguru—keep these in your hands."

"You really think they'll be useful?" Jean joked.

"Yes, yes, yes. Very solid."

A little way outside the district limits, at a crossing of two trails, he prostrated himself on the ground, his arms crossed, and rested there for several minutes.

We reached Eyssenazu, the first village within the Ulamai district. The inhabitants blocked our passage across the square. Voiné argued at length with them. We sat in the shade of a hut's awning. The men watched us with distrustful eyes. Voiné made a tour of the village, talking away at the doors of huts. Finally he rejoined us, his head bowed.

"Well?"

"It would be better if I didn't go any farther," he said. "The Toma, if you force their hand, become very nasty. You'll have to be careful."

"You want to stay here?"

"It would be very hot for me, over at Soguru. You, you're white men. You can go ahead."

We did not insist. We asked for another guide. Contrary to our expectations, the natives selected a man to go with us. Then Voiné changed his mind; he got himself in hand again and led the column.

The usual direct road to Soguru crossed the initiation forest a little beyond where we were. To avoid antagonizing the witch-doctors, we took a detour, much longer and much harder going.

In a small village unfamiliar to us, we found the messenger in leggings. He was waiting for us. Tired, we sprawled on the ground. At the other end of the village the dignitaries, squatting, watched us carefully. But none rose to come and greet us. According to the messenger, the master of the tattooing and the district chief had preceded us.

"The master of the tattooing?" I said to Voiné. "But I thought that was Zézé, in Soguru."

"Not any more," Voiné said with a helpless gesture. "They changed."

That brutal destitution spoke volumes on the bitterness of the enemy faction.

But Voiné had conquered his fear and wanted to have done with all this as soon as possible. He was impatient and urged us to hurry. For him, this was all maneuvering. If we really wanted to see the chief, we had to go directly to where he was. The man in leggings did not share that opinion, but agreed to guide us along a new trail that detoured around the sacred wood. Roughly cleared, it bristled with sharp stumps of saplings slashed by machetes. Voiné set a fast pace. We did not want to fall behind. Barefoot on the hills and abrupt descents, we cut ourselves at every step.

"Now they take us for fakirs," Jean growled, in bad temper.

A stream some hundred yards across cut off the trail. We floundered in the mud, taking huge strides, out of breath, feet bloody. After three hours of this calvary we moved onto a wide trail that should, Voiné said, have us in Soguru within fifteen minutes.

From the bush very close by rose suddenly the harsh scream of the Afwi. I stopped; through the lacework of lianas and branches I glimpsed the figures of men; among them stood the great black mask.

"Quick, quick!" screamed our guide, who broke into a run toward the village.

Without knowing why, we followed him. We had seen the Afwi before; we were tattooed. Why should we flee from the Great Spirit? Behind us the sacred music left off; we dropped to a normal pace.

The trail sloped steadily downhill. Between the trees, roofs appeared: Soguru. It was the first Toma village I had seen built in a hollow and not at the flat peak of a hill. A few strings of blue smoke rose through the tranquil air. Soguru was a large village. I noticed, with surprise, several square huts. We came closer. Everything was deserted, silent. No women before their huts. No elders.

We had hardly crossed the circle of lianas when, from all sides, men surged out at us, hard-faced: they surrounded us immediately. I asked Voiné to request a hut where we could rest, and some water. This was customary. No one answered. The hostile circle narrowed. We sat down where we were and tried to preserve a casual air.

Finally the district chief arrived. He addressed us in Toma, when he knew French perfectly well, and asked Voiné to translate.

The elders' decision was irrevocable: they refused definitively to let us film anything at all. The secrets of the Toma were not for the whites. They declared themselves ready to help us in any other way, but they would reveal no more secrets.

Without much hope, I tried to make our intentions more precise. We had never used force or deceit to learn the mysteries of the

sacred wood. Certain Toma had shown them to us because we were
their friends and because they trusted us. We had promised to reveal
nothing to the Toma women or to the Bilakoro. We would never
show our film in black Africa, and we were ready to put our promises
into writing once more, to sign a contract with them. If they permitted us to attend the festivities, we would film only what they authorized.

An old man stepped forward then. I did not recognize him. "The
master of the tattooing," Voiné whispered. He ordered the men to
withdraw to the forest for deliberations, spoke briefly to Voiné in
cutting tones, and left.

There we were again, alone in the deserted village. Voiné was
gray with fear. "The old man said that I was the one who brought
you here, so I would die and you too."

Jean and I looked at each other.

There were three of us, unarmed. It was impossible to predict the
next few hours. Most important, we ought not to show nervousness.
We had only one way to impress them: by remaining calm.

Jean stood up and loaded his Leica with careful, precise motions.
His eye to the view-finder, he waited.

A growing hubbub surrounded us. The square was still empty.
I felt a tiny pinch at my heart.

"That's it," Voiné stammered. "That's it. They're coming to
kill us."

In no time at all we were ringed by a mob of Toma. There must
have been almost three hundred of them. Their impassivity contrasted with their fury a short time before; I was even less confident.

CHAPTER ELEVEN

Fichter, unemotional, snapped photo after photo. When a long silence had ended, the district chief translated the old man's words for me:

"If you remain here," he said, "the men will remain around you. You will be unable to move. You will have neither hut nor water nor fire."

Voiné begged us not to insist. "Let's go now, *patron*. Let's go now."

Regretfully we beat our retreat. We had no choice. A dozen men remained around us. They escorted us silently to the nearest village; but once we had crossed the circle of lianas, they lost their fierce expressions. When they left us, we exchanged brief good-bys with them: *"Gueria. . . . Gueriao. . . ."*

Now and then we passed a group of Toma, certainly informed of the incident. They stopped what they were doing to watch us go by. Some stared ironically at us; others, to the contrary, extended their hands in the ritual greeting and threw us sympathetic glances.

Day was drawing to an end. Dead tired, our feet in a pitiful state, we were obliged to stop in a hamlet well before Tuwelu. Tony was there, on his way to join us with the flares. He was so sure of our success that he had prepared, among other things, gifts for the natives of Tuwelu. To celebrate the successful completion of the film he had brought along a few bottles of vintage wine, a Camembert, and a sausage, products that we had learned to do without since our arrival in Toma country.

In the hut left at our disposal we shared the banquet with Voiné, and consoled ourselves as well as we could for our blighted hopes.

Toward the middle of the night Jean's groans woke us. He was shaking with fever; his stomach racked him atrociously. He twisted in pain, to the point where we found it necessary to stretch him out on a mat; it was impossible to trust him in a hammock. He was seized with spasmodic retching and went through a violent attack of dysentery. We searched through the pharmacy crate. Whatever he had, a sedative was in order. Until morning he went on groaning, rolling on his mat, and we could do nothing for him. Voiné, terrified, kept repeating: "It's the Soguru people. . . . *Patron,* they poisoned him!"

We decided to have Jean carried in his hammock, but when the time came to leave he felt slightly better and refused the improvised transport energetically. Tony and I stayed behind to supervise the bearers' departure. Jean and Voiné went ahead.

We caught up with them soon. Pallid, his eyes glazed and hollow, Jean was trying to ford a stream, hanging on Voiné's shoulder. Up to the waist in muddy water, he was wearing himself out; but he insisted that he wanted to walk.

A quarter of a mile from the village, in the shadow of the high black bluff of Oko, Jean was overtaken by an attack of uncontrollable vomiting. Tony and I supported him, each under one arm, and we climbed slowly up the long hillside toward the entrance to Tuwelu. Women who were preparing meals, old men who had been lazing in front of their huts, children, all approached. The silent, anxious crowd formed a lane to our hut.

We slipped an exhausted Jean into his sleeping-bag and laid him out on a mat.

CHAPTER ELEVEN

Now we had to face reality. We had no idea what was wrong with him, and we were incapable of curing him. The natives had grouped around the doorway, grieved and worried, not daring to speak. In the darkened hut Jean jerked in spasms, racked by intolerable pain, his face waxy.

Old Zézé arrived from the sacred wood, breathing hard. He examined Jean, palpated him very gently, and disappeared after a brief conversation with Voiné. A few moments later he reappeared, solemn, closed the door of the hut, and pulled a long cotton bag from the folds of his tunic. Awkwardly he drew an earthenware vessel from it, covered with dried blood and cowrie shells; he uncorked the vessel, inserted a narrow stick, and licked at a whitish viscous liquid that gave off a nauseating odor. By that he wanted to prove that there was nothing to fear. We shook Jean.

"Old Zézé's going to dose you," Voiné told him.

In the smallest of voices Jean asked my opinion. "Would you take it?"

"There's nothing else to be done. You never know."

We held him up so that he could swallow the horrible potion. He opened his mouth, swallowed, and grimaced fearfully.

"It's poison," he murmured. "If I don't die of it . . ."

After a short spell of calm the painful spasms took hold again, even worse than before; Jean became weaker by the minute. Tony and I decided to have him carried to the roadside in his hammock, and from there to put him in a truck headed for the nearest European center.

But when he saw the eight bearers and the palanquin arrive, he refused to move; he stiffened himself mightily against the pain, and succeeded only in aggravating it. I helped him sit up.

"It may only be amœbic dysentery, Jean, but you'll have to go. You can come back when it's passed."

He looked at me. In one night he had become unrecognizable. Finally he yielded.

The men spelled each other in teams of four. The hammock, a few yards from me, swung between the naked gleaming torsos of the bearers. On steep grades, up or down, the men slid on the sticky clay of the trail, and Jean found himself at times with his feet higher than his head. To cross streams, all eight men had to take a hand. I saw Jean's chalky face, the nose pinched, the lips bloodless. For him this trip must have been torture.

When we marched through villages the inhabitants came out to watch us pass, not speaking, looking their compassion, like the natives of Tuwelu.

Several times I thought Jean had fainted; I ran to his side and shook him; but each time he reassured me in a feeble voice: "No, it's all right for the moment. I think I can hold out."

At Bofosso we found ourselves back in the little hut across from Baré's. This was the third expedition Jean and I had made together. We had never yet been separated. Now we waited two or three hours. We had not much to say to each other. I made a bundle of his things.

Finally a truck arrived, driven by a white. I hoisted Jean up beside the driver. He said something about joining us as soon as he was back on his feet. I knew that Soguru was the final goal for him too, and that he couldn't admit the idea that the film might remain unfinished. But I ordered him to go directly back to France.

"Tony and I can handle whatever's left to be done."

The truck started up. I threw a last look at Jean, crumpled on the front seat, his gaze dulled, his head thrown back.

I watched the truck move away. I was not too sure what would become of Jean now . . . but I had no time to linger over the thought. There might still be a chance of finishing our work, and Tony was waiting for me in Tuwelu.

TWELVE

I came back alone. Once Jean was in the truck, the bearers had scattered. My nerves twitching, I hiked through villages, across streams, through the bush, through the savanna, like a somnambulist. I was so exhausted that I could hardly feel my own fatigue. I thought about nothing. I walked. A phrase chased itself through my brain: "Have to shoot the tattooing. . . ." I hung on to that idea as if it were a question of life or death.

A storm swung low over me, hovered in the night sky, and drifted off in another direction, detoured by a capricious wind. Full night overtook me in the low savanna beyond Serissu. I forgot to worry about getting lost.

My arrival in Tuwelu surprised no one. The whole village lay plunged in a sort of torpor. Through the open doors of huts I saw the gleam of fires.

Tony was eating, pensively. Voiné and Zézé, silent, were sitting beside him. All three looked up when I came in. They had not expected me tonight.

"How's Jean?"

"I hope he holds out. He wasn't any better when I put him on the truck."

I told them about the trip in a few words. While I was gone Tony had taken photographs in the village and recorded women's songs new to us. I told him how I felt about doing everything possible to attend the Soguru ceremonies. He agreed immediately. Whatever happened would happen within the next few days.

Zézé, who had been listening but not understanding, came out of his silence. "I promised to take you to Soguru, and I'll do it. I'll go in ahead of you, to chase away the evil charms they put in your path."

"But do you think they'll let us know the date of the ceremony?"

"They'll have to. We've already made gifts to the Guelemlai. They have to tell the whole Toma country. We'll leave with the men, covered with banana leaves, and get there the day of the tattooing."

The voices of the two witch-doctors echoed gloomily, without timbre. They wanted to keep their promises and nothing more.

Bulls galloped from one end of the village to the other all night, lowing ferociously. Occasionally they crowded up against the wall of the hut under the awning. We heard their heavy breathing, the scrape of their backs against the wall. We couldn't sleep; at a loss, we exchanged brief phrases over the dim lantern-light.

"There was a panther outside the village last night," Voiné said tonelessly, entering the hut. The animals had been frightened.

We wandered through the village half the next morning; then, in revolt against inaction, we decided to do something, anything for the sake of doing something, and asked Voiné to lead us to the cave where the ancestors' spirits assembled, near Doezia. He had spoken of this holy place for some time, but up to now had consistently refused to take us there. Today he agreed immediately, but with one condition: that no one know. We would go alone with him and skirt the villages.

A fine drizzle had set in. No matter; we'd be drenched if we had to, but we wouldn't wait. Voiné made no objection.

A little before reaching Doezia we cut off the trail and moved through the solid bush. There was no visible trace of a passage, but Voiné, very sure of the path, windmilled his way through with a machete. We fought shrubbery and dripping lianas; we clutched thorny branches to avoid the quicksand beds of streams; and in that fight against the trail, under the rain, we managed to forget our troubles for a while.

A subforest, relatively clear, succeeded to the choked bush; very high above us was the arch of dense leaves. Enormous trunks matted with slabs of moss shot up straight all around us; a carpet of humus deadened all sound. In the green shadow at the end of a kind of lane we noticed a smooth wall of black rock, in which a wide triangular mouth opened.

"That's it," Voiné said.

He led us inside. There was a deep semicircular room divided in two by a huge boulder fallen from the ceiling. In almost total darkness I made out a pile of *guinzé* and pottery on flat bloodstained rocks.

"They kill a bull here for all the big celebrations, and every new district chief has to come here to honor his ancestors," Voiné said.

We looked for traces of frescoes on the walls. There was nothing; the cavern was bare, somber, sinister. We remained for a moment, silent. Outside, the heavy rainfall had become a gentle spring drizzle again. Voiné was sitting on a rock deep in the grotto.

He had first led us freely to the cavern where the spirit of Vevego,

Zézé's ancestor, lived; then, hesitantly, to the grotto of the ancestors in Kovabakoro; and today he had violated ancestral taboos once more to lead us to this place where all the spirits assembled. I saw the standing tombstones, spattered with the violet meat of ground kola nuts; the sacrificial altars stained by the blood of victims. And for the first time I understood all the importance attached by the Toma to ancestor-worship; it was under the ægis of the ancestors that all important acts of Toma existence were performed.

Toward the end of the valley, a little lower down, we found ourselves under a rocky overhang some fifty yards long. Intricately laced lianas wove a thick net between the bush and the arch. Two small birds of prey, featherless, fell cheeping to earth. Voiné picked them up and stuffed them into the slash pocket of his tunic. Then he showed us the debris of some black pottery in a corner.

"This is where the boys come to learn how to make the Afwi speak." He swept his glance across the shelter hollowed out of rock. "In the time of force those who fought the whites hid themselves here. The cannon couldn't get them here. Even a plane couldn't."

"You know," I said, "the whites have invented machines now that can break through anything."

Voiné stood lost in thought for a moment.

"That's too much!" he said finally.

We went back toward Tuwelu. The rain was a downpour again.

Brutally, suddenly, Tony was gripped by a terrible colic. He developed the same symptoms Jean had shown. In a short while his face became hollow, flaccid. Voiné, panicky, was no help. In his eyes, the malediction of the spirits was upon us. Tony, doubled over, hands on his belly, shuffled as he walked, dragging his feet, tense with pain. Voiné and I helped him as much as possible over the last few miles between us and Tuwelu.

I wanted to call the bearers together so that he could leave by hammock that same night, but the men were dead set against marching in darkness under a driving rain, and Tony, like Jean, held out grimly against that course of action. Voiné and I had laid him down in the dark hut. I leaned over him.

"Give me medicine," he said feebly.

I opened the case and looked for a sedative, something to relieve his pain. He was ready to try anything. But for him as for Jean, there was nothing I could do.

All night he had cramps, was convulsed on his mat, vomited. Zézé, Voiné, and I spelled each other at his bedside, unable to help him. The master witch-doctor did not even try to administer his own home-made antidotes. At dawn Tony's suffering had not diminished. This time he resigned himself to leaving. He would follow the same route Jean had followed, going back to the main road and from there to Macenta. But he insisted that I stay behind. He'd be all right by himself. And I couldn't abandon all the equipment, or even lose so much as one day, before finishing the work we had begun together.

It was a hard decision to make, but I knew he was right; I didn't insist. Then I went to find Voiné, with a new idea but with no rosy illusions. I expected his refusal.

"I could feel their gri-gris," he said. "They've turned all their evil powers against us. The two *patrons* are sick. We can't go back."

"You really don't want to go?"

He shook his head. "But you felt it too. It's impossible," he said, with a hysterical look. "You could feel all the gri-gris that breathe!"

I could hardly be angry.

Zézé made no objection to a last try, but said nothing about preceding me. For him, to go to Soguru would be suicide.

There was only an infinitesimal hope, but I was beginning to acquire a deep understanding of Toma reactions. Perhaps seeing me come back alone, empty-handed, after my friends had been struck down, they would accept me as one of themselves. If there remained the slightest chance to film the great tattooing ceremonies, I had no right to pass it up. Jean had told me that, and Tony had repeated it after him.

But Voiné's words and Zézé's worries had shaken me up a bit, and I felt a little reluctance. I went from group to group. The men of the village would have liked to help me. But that they go to Soguru was too much to ask. Finally I managed to convince a friend of Voiné's, a man named Akoi, a pleasant old drunkard with a perpetual toothless smile, who knew a few words of French. He was ready to leave right away. He was half irresponsible, an innocent; even the men of Soguru would not be capable of harming him.

The bearers started out. Tony lay in his hammock; his face was white. Voiné would accompany him as far as Bofosso. I went out to the village limits with them. Gesturing feebly, Tony said good-by to me. I watched the palanquin sway along the downhill trail; Voiné's black hat disappeared among the trees.

For a long moment I stood motionless, facing the bush that had swallowed up my two companions a few days apart. Then I went back to the village, signaled to Akoi, who was waiting for me in a state of bliss, and we struck out in the opposite direction, toward Soguru. Happily, the rain had let up, but the previous night's storms had left their mark on the whole forest. Streams were overflowing, and the slippery clay trail was overlaid by a tangle of broken branches.

We made a short halt in a village; I sat back against a hut. The ground and the thatched roofs were covered with dead leaves, or leaves only recently ripped from their boughs. I had not seen the Toma country under that aspect before. A vague oppression filled me. I felt a growing desire to remain where I was, to go no farther. Slowly I walked around the village. All life seemed extinct. I approached the huts. The elders themselves were absent. We were absolutely alone, Akoi and I. The ceremonies at Soguru must have begun. That thought pulled me abruptly out of my inertia. I straightened up; followed by the faithful Akoi I went on to Eyssenazu, scarcely conscious of time and distance.

There, at Eyssenazu, began the great initiation forest. I stopped, hesitated. I sat down on a flat tombstone, and almost immediately a group of witch-doctors (I recognized them by their curved tridents) stepped toward me. I knew none of these old men. They did not seem dangerous. One of them gave me a handful of kola nuts, all red; and I remembered Voiné's warning: "If there isn't even one white nut, the man who gave them to you wants to poison you."

The way things were now, I couldn't hesitate. I split a nut down the middle and gave the old man half. With a wide smile, he nibbled on his as I nibbled mine.

No one understood French. I wrote a note to the district chief and the master of the initiation, asking them to come to meet me here. And I managed to explain that Akoi would take it into Soguru. They agreed after a moment of deliberation, but it was obvious that they would not permit me to enter the village myself.

Long hours of waiting began. Three old men sat down beside me and tried to work up a conversation. My Toma vocabulary was very sparse. To prove the innocence of their intentions, they brought me more gifts: bananas, mangoes, gourds of cool water.

Thick, dazzlingly white clouds scudded across the bright sky. Nothing moved in the village. I was there among all those silent old men. I knew that the die had been cast, and that I had lost the last throw. Tomorrow, perhaps, I would leave the Toma country, and I might never come back. I was already nostalgic. I looked at the tombs, the round huts with their black paintings, the high wall of forest, the whole familiar setting, as though I would never see it all again.

The two messengers arrived within a few minutes of each other. The one from the district commander in Macenta thought I was in Soguru. The letter was brief: we were to suspend our movie-making because of the troubles it might give rise to in the region. The order was formal. The usual messenger from the district chief, the man in leggings, brought an almost illegible note. With considerable difficulty I deciphered it. As soon as the ceremony was over, the chiefs and the elders would grant us free access to the district and would help us all they could. We already knew all the Toma secrets; what more could we want? "If you come now," it said in essence, "we'll have to interrupt the tattooing. The spirits of the ancestors will be angry, and we will all die. But we refuse to show you anything more. We prefer to die."

It was useless to fight back. I reassured the two messengers. I would make no attempt to go to Soguru. Now all I felt was a great lassitude. The idea of retreating, of spending the night in Tuwelu, was almost sickening, but I had no choice now. The old men shook hands with me in Toma fashion. They had succeeded in halting me; yet they seemed rather saddened than triumphant.

Akoi had not come back. I walked with mechanical steps. Night fell over the murmuring forest. I had never felt so alone. After a while I decided that I must be lost, and sat down at the roadside, exhausted. But Akoi ambled up, whistling as far off-key as possible, glanced at me without speaking, and went on ahead. A little relieved, I picked myself up and followed him. In a small basket on his head he was carrying the same gifts the witch-doctors had given me. Suddenly he turned and struck himself on the chest.

"Akoi, Soguru, very bad."

I didn't understand too well.

He repeated: "Voiné, Zézé, Akoi, Soguru very bad."

I thought I grasped his meaning, but his naïve smile seemed to belie what he had just said. I would have my explanation in Tuwelu.

Zézé and Voiné came into my hut and sat down wordlessly. I thought I knew them well, but I had never seen them as they were tonight. Voiné was stiff, solemn, his eyes protruding; Zézé seemed older, more hunched than usual. Then Zézé straightened slowly and began to speak in a slightly broken voice. He stopped after each sentence to let Voiné translate.

CHAPTER TWELVE

"At Soguru the witch-doctors said: 'Zézé was the strongest, but he gave our secrets to the whites. He let them be eaten by the Afwi and now they bear the trace of his teeth on their bodies forever, like Toma, and that is not possible. A white man is a white man, and a black man is a black man. Voiné, who guided the whites, Wego, who helped them, Akoi, and all the men of Tuwelu who showed them the Afwi are equally guilty. Zézé, Voiné, and Wego will go to Soguru when the whites have left, and they will be judged.' " Then he was still.

I asked: "Will you go?"

"I am a pure Toma," Voiné answered. "There is no life for me outside my own country. I must go."

"If a man has done something that he ought to be ashamed of," Zézé said, "it would be better that he die right away. I will go."

Wego had come in and was sitting in a shadowed corner. He had not spoken, but there could be no question in his case.

"I'll do all I can to protect you," I said to Voiné.

"There's nothing you can do," Zézé said. "This is an affair for the Toma alone. You did nothing by force. You didn't deceive us. We can't be sorry for what has been done. There is nothing to reproach us for, so we will be the stronger at the trial. Tomorrow the village will give you bearers, and we'll come with you to Bofosso."

We shared a meal in silence. The village knew all about it now. A few old women brought us kola nuts. All the dignitaries, all the elders, came to sit with us. Outside the door, the eyes of women and children gleamed in the night. They did not want to leave me by myself.

THIRTEEN

I watched these three men sitting with their backs to the wall: Zézé, Voiné, Wego, baffled, their eyes dulled. I had wanted to unveil the secrets of the Toma; I had expected to find that these witch-doctors were beings apart; and tonight, in their reactions, in their fear, I saw that they were simply men.

I had arrived here with a head full of logic, with a need to label, to classify. I had sought the why of everything, without being willing to admit that the Toma lived in a world of relationships different from our own. "Because it's that way," they answered; or they gave me their own reasons, which could never satisfy me. I insisted; often I suggested, without realizing it myself, possible solutions; they always ended by choosing one, either because they found it more attractive or, more simply, to please me and end the questioning.

I was constantly coming up against contradictions that never bothered them. All those forest spirits—even the witch-doctors admitted that they were man-made—those charms, base commodities, those masks, that love of the secret for its own sake, all that disappointed me a bit; I saw nothing but tricks all around me.

I had wanted to find an inhuman purity and rigor among the Toma.

The predicted lightning in Doezia and the series of Voinés in Sagpaou, inexplicable on the surface, were almost certainly part of a body of phenomena of premonition, of suggestion, so far investigated only superficially, but the existence of which cannot be denied. I had not been at all surprised to find them among the most instinctive of men, more attentive than we to dreams, to coincidences, to all obscure forces.

In my confusion, I had expected other things of them; but the attitude of the three witch-doctors tonight, and of the men of Soguru, was forcing me to see more clearly.

The first problem to resist solution was that of the creation of man. The Toma make no more attempt to explain that than they do to define the afterlife; yet they believe in the afterlife, as my visit to the cavern inhabited by ancestral spirits proved. We saw time and time again that they were convinced of the existence of phantoms; they spoke constantly of the spirits. But what did that word mean in their mouths?

I pictured the gateway to the initiation camp in Niogbozu, and the effigies of spirits under the small awning. We surely had a photograph of it taken the year before. I shuffled through our reports and documents and found it. The Toma cosmogony was there before my eyes. I had not been able to work it out previously because I had not known Okobuzogui, the secret mask, incarnation of the Afwi. Today I identified him easily by the great X that crossed his face, distinguishing him from all other incarnations. To his left a man, a woman, and a beast were seated, in that order. They were set back against a wall on which the great serpent twined among painted black patterns. It could all be explained now; it was so simple that I had never thought of it before.

"In the beginning," Zézé had said, "there was the water, the serpent, the Belimassai, and the Zazi." At first I was tempted to believe that these were symbols of the four elements: water, earth, air, and fire; but probably they represent an analogous structure. The water was what existed below, matter; the thunderstone was the sky, from which the first medicines came; the serpent was the link between the two, the first manifestation of life, prelude to man's appearance.

This scheme, plus the presence of Okobuzogui, gave me the significance of the masks. Okobuzogui, secret incarnation of the Afwi, dedicated as his name implies to the great witch-doctor hero and founder of the village, symbolized occult power. The pair of Bakorogui, male and female, stood for the human being, with the hierarchy and separation of the sexes, the basis of Toma society. The animal world appeared in Angbai, "laden with skins," and the Wenilegagui, "laden with feathers."

Laniboi occupied a place apart; Voiné had explained it to me. "Long ago, all men were as tall as the Laniboi." It was probable that they were a symbol of temporal power, of the warrior-ancestor, like old Kréan.

I could have spent considerable time tracing the origin of the masks; it was lost, like the origin of man, in the deep night of time. The Afwi himself was the union of all Toma. It was not *he* who had created *them;* as Zézé said, "We, the Zogui, made all that." That phrase, taken in its literal sense, had crowned my disappointment. But he was speaking only of the masks, the talismans, the exterior forms of a religion designed to maintain the tradition of which he, the Zogui, was guardian. Without those symbols and those strange rites, the religion would disappear, and with it the social structure of which it was the expression. Deprived of the ancestral traditions, the Toma believe, they would be unable to survive.

The witch-doctors had not lied to me when, having let us hear the voice of the Great Spirit of the sacred wood, they said: "That is the great rite, the great secret that no white man may know." The voice, the Word, that makes man a different and higher being, is the only manifestation of the Afwi, the Supreme Being, that contains all the symbols of the Toma cosmogony. "The Afwi is the union of all the Toma." He became a kind of abstraction to me, and yet I knew very well that for the Toma he is inseparable from his other manifestations. Long, long ago, men, the ancestors of the Toma, who had come together from all points, according to Voiné, grouped to defend themselves against the forest and against other men. This is not a unique case. The Boni and the Nyuga of French Guiana had constructed a similar cosmogony, which allowed them to survive in the forests of the upper Maroni when, escaped Negro slaves, they had arrived there from all over Africa. The Toma had understood that their very existence depended on unity, and they made a kind of divinity of it, the Afwi, the highest being, symbol of collectivity, who devoured the young males to integrate them into the tribe, and to whom a human being was occasionally sacrificed, to supply him with the vigor of fresh blood.

The rites of the sacred wood conform strictly to this symbolism. The young Toma, at the time of his initiation, is granted a revelation of that great collective force. He renounces his individuality to become part of the Toma community, which participates in the

Afwi, the Spirit; and he identifies himself with the beasts through his animal totem.

But the strength of that tradition lies in secrecy: it is an occultism that cuts off the Toma from all exchange with the outside world, and thus imposes a limit to their level of civilization. Their religion is a religion of the Toma for the Toma.

Even now, contacts are being established everywhere with other tribes and with the whites: the Toma are being forced out of their isolation. The forest has become less hostile and the occult less indispensable in regard to foreigners. The three men who helped us felt this in a confused way and revealed their secrets to us; but what our civilization brings to the Toma cannot be adapted to their present needs.

That is why the witch-doctors assembled at Soguru closed the breach opened in the wall of the Sacred Wood.

We had arrived full of good will, ready to undergo anything for fuller understanding; but they knew well that we were not going to build our own huts, cultivate our own *lugans*, and integrate ourselves definitively into their community. We accepted all the outer forms, but not the real consequences of our initiation.

"Now you know our secrets," they said rightly. "What more do you want?"

Zézé and Voiné, by their actions, had placed themselves outside the Collectivity, and they were afraid of it; they were afraid too of the uncontrollable forces that any act of that kind might loose. Our arrival and the incident we caused had upset the ancestral order

CHAPTER THIRTEEN

231

of life and had obliged the Toma to ask themselves unanswerable questions, questions they had avoided raising until now.

But I reminded myself that I was analyzing it all with a white man's logic. For them, the Toma, these symbols live, contradict one another, overlap one another, and cannot be so simply classified.

There was no way they could explain it to me. I had to understand it alone.

FOURTEEN

"Don't worry about bearers," Voiné said to me. "The equipment will come along after you."

All the natives of Tuwelu had walked out to the circle of lianas. Their faces sorrowful, they were silent. Many of them shook hands with me in white man's fashion. The children watched me with wide, serious eyes. I did not want to leave, but I knew very well that I could do nothing more here. A drab sky hung heavily over the bush. For the last time we dropped down the trail to Bofosso.

The three witch-doctors preceded me in silence. This time I could not tire of contemplating the Toma country; it was as though I were afraid of forgetting. We passed several *lugans*. In the black earth burned away by clearing operations, where great limed trunks rose here and there, the first tender green shoots of rice were pushing up. The men had built temporary palm huts near the *lugans*, where the guard, who chased off rapacious birds, could live with his family. As we walked, men came to the edge of the trail to greet us. The ritual slapping of fingers was still friendly, but I felt that an invisible bond was already broken. Behind me Toma life went on, immutable.

When we reached Bofosso, I went to Baré's hut. Over the door hung a sign that Jean, Tony, and I had made for him: *A la Tour d'Argent, Gargote no 1. Baré, propriétaire à Bofosso.*

In shorts and a blue apron, Baré was filling a demijohn of wine from the barrel with a rubber hose. He straightened up and smiled.

"Ah, *patron*! I thought you were dead."

"And Tony?"

"I saw him. He was pretty sick. He left for Macenta."

Baré went to get two glasses and filled them. We gossiped.

"And the film?" he asked.

"You know what happened."

"Yes. Those people in Soguru, they're not a bad bunch. They just don't understand things, that's all."

"Maybe," I said, shrugging. "It's not important now."

I didn't want to talk to Baré. I felt empty, as though I were coming out of a nightmare.

Dusk came. It was too late to leave for Macenta tonight. Anyway, there was no truck.

I set up my hammock in our old hut across from the *gargote*. The pit had already been dug between me and the witch-doctors. They had withdrawn to Voiné's hut at the other end of the village, and I ate alone, squatting on the Toma bed.

After the meal I waited for their visit, but they did not show up for the usual long evening of talk. They had nothing more to say to me. They were afraid to see me go, and at the same time wanted to hasten my departure. Afterward they would be alone with their hostile brothers. "This is an affair of the Toma alone."

In the lamplight I went through my script notes, and discovered that, thanks to the failure at Soguru, several backgrounds were lacking. Impossible to shoot them alone. I tried all possible combinations in montage, and found always the same insoluble problems. Tomorrow morning I would send word to Tony to join me if he could.

THE SACRED FOREST

Since dawn I had been pacing up and down at the roadside. I had scribbled a quick note to Tony, full of big words and exhortation: last-minute burst of energy, work to be done at any cost, an effort of will. . . . I had known that pomposity and emphasis would be unnecessary, that Tony would come anyway; but in my state of nervous debilitation I had let out all stops.

Suddenly a five-ton truck, coming up from Macenta, skidded to a halt before the hut, in a cloud of yellow dust. An African driver in a flowered shirt jumped out of the cab and tipped his hat very politely.

"Excuse me, sir. You wouldn't have any strong glue, would you?"

I stared at him, dumbfounded.

"No," I said, "not here."

With a vague word of thanks and a wide salute, he scrambled back into the cab and took off.

I recovered slowly from this onslaught of absurdity. Even if the truck had turned back to Macenta, I would certainly have forgotten to give the driver my letter. About two hours later a native trucker agreed to run the errand for me.

I wandered around Bofosso and went to Voiné's hut several times; Zézé and Wego were there, collapsed in their hammocks, inert. Voiné pretended to be sleeping on his mat; he was facing the wall. I sat down near him and shook him gently.

"Voiné, I asked Tony to come out. I'm waiting for him now."

Voiné sat up. "But he's sick!"

"I hope he can come anyway. And I'll need you for the shooting."

Voiné got up and we walked through the village together. We

stopped at Baré's place and had a glass of wine. Then we took up our vigil at the roadside. Voiné was taciturn. I offered him a cigarette and we smoked without speaking.

A luxurious bush-car roared up the Guekedu road and screeched to a halt in front of Baré's. A front door opened. A colonel got out. The other front door swung open. A second colonel stepped out. At the rear doors two more colonels appeared simultaneously. With my nerves as bad as they were, I thought for a moment that I was in the grip of another hallucination. I looked at Voiné. He was considering the uniforms.

The four officers threw a rapid glance in my direction; one of them went into Baré's. He came out almost immediately and announced: "Nothing here," and the four of them, officers in the public health service, probably on an inspection tour, climbed back into the station-wagon and left.

"The red ears," Voiné said.

"Red ears?"

"During the time of force, the Toma called them that."

These first two contacts of the day with civilization revisited left me somewhat perplexed for a while.

Late in the afternoon a truck stopped at the roadside and Tony stepped down, staggering so that I had to support him. Now I was remorseful for having sent for him. He claimed to be much better, but could hardly stand up and could take no food at all.

After a painful night on his part we tried to shoot the necessary backgrounds. Between every two operations Tony had to lie down, and our actors, the witch-doctors, who were no longer even slightly interested in the work, were very little help to us. Half-heartedly they posed. Enthusiasm was at a low ebb.

The forest had never been as luxuriant, the colors in the Bofosso market place had never been as dazzling, under a clear sky and a finally bright sun. Was it to make us regret leaving even more? In a few moments we would quit the Toma country on one of the market trucks.

Baré's assistants loaded the last crates on the rear platform. This spectacle attracted great numbers of the curious; but suddenly the crowd split, making way for a man of imposing stature. He had a kind of elongated sickle in one hand, something like the weapon once used by the druids to cut the sacred mistletoe. I recognized him by that magical appurtenance: it was Darazu Koiwogui, Zézé's rival, the charlatan of Anorezia who had succeeded in barring us from the sacred wood. Impassive, he extended his hand. I don't know why we did, but we shook hands with him. Then he turned away and left without a word.

The motor turned over. The driver was waiting for us. Instinctively our friends came closer; we formed a compact group; no one wanted to begin drawing away.

"The forest spirits will help you . . . even in France," Zézé said.

Voiné could not release my hand. Wego's face lost its immobility for a moment. Tony and I jumped to the platform, the truck moved forward, and soon all we could see was three motionless silhouettes against the colorful crowd.

CHAPTER FOURTEEN

Bofosso disappeared. Outside the village we passed a lone man: it was Vuriakoli, the first to have refused us Toma secrets. He recognized us, too, and raised his trident.

The forest seemed to close in above the road. A vast storm-front filled the Toma sky.

APPENDIX

The texts brought together in this appendix are, with the exception of the press clipping, Voiné's words, taken down as he spoke.

]

TO MAKE A MASK LIKE ANGBAI

You must make the sacrifice on the buloi tree.

One egg, two *guinzés*, seven balls of ground rice, a rolled mat, a white kola nut, a red kola nut. You pile everything up, you say your name. You cleave the tree with your hatchet, and say to the tree:

If you accept the gift, you give me wealth.

If the hatchet has fallen the next day, that means the tree has not agreed that you be its fiancé.

Because when you have a fiancée, you give her three strips of tunic cloth, kola nuts, and *guinzés*.

If the hatchet has not fallen, then you prepare the wood and you let it dry for a month. If you do not know how to carve the mask, you give the wood to the blacksmith.* Then the witch-doctors put sacred leaves on the wood. You give them a chicken for going out into the bush and a chicken for curing the owner of the gri-gri, seventeen *guinzés*, seven kola nuts, one yard of white tunic cloth, one yard of striped, and one yard of yellow.

You sew the bands together on the long sides and you give them to the old witch-doctor who saw to it that the hatchet did not fall.

Plus a gourd full of rice.

* The Toma blacksmith is also the basket-weaver and carpenter.

Plus a gourd full of palm oil.

Plus a gourd full of dried meat.

Plus two pounds of salt.

Then the witch-doctor asks for a cock, which he kills on the gri-gri when he gives his name.

Because at night the gri-gri, in dreams, comes to tell its name to each man.

The witch-doctors say that you must marry a woman after you marry the gri-gri.

So you give 207 bundles of *guinzé*, a red cock, and a white cock.

If you are a witch-doctor, as long as you are not married to a gri-gri you cannot win a woman.

When the gri-gri has given its name, it helps you to the end of your life.

2

THE MEANING OF PLACE-NAMES

Niogbozu: Line up.

Bofosso: Where there are many lianas and shadows.

Tuwelu: Where there are many kola trees.

Bogbozu: Where there is much twisted liana.

Gueriguerika: The region where people are very wise.

Bobokozu: The region where bees sting much.

Kotezia: The region where you find white paintings.

Baguromai: The region where when people say no, it means no.

Serinke: The place in equilibrium.

Doezia: Where everyone must go.

Voribassu: Where they pray for good business and things go well.

APPENDIX

Ferezia: Where there are partridges and where you do evil with no consequences and good similarly.

Vorua: Where the moon brightens the night most. And if you give birth to a son there, he will become a chief.

Tainama: Where the people lie too much.

Fassazu: Where the big rock is.

Singuega: Where the elephant was.

Anorezia: Where all the devils come.

Sebuamai: Where you dream well.

Surogozu: Where sentinels are picketed in case of war.

Soguru: Where there are many sorcerers.

3

THE STORY OF OLD KRÉAN

The old Massawai was marching with all his warriors, his women, his children, etc. . . . .

Each time that he stopped at a place in the Kolibiramatoma, he named the place. You still see traces of him where he sat on a rock and where he stuck his knife into the stone.

The warriors of old Kréan were not happy about the arrival of Massawai.

Then, to calm them, old Kréan, who flew around at night with fire in his hand, went before Massawai and said to him: "Why have you come to this country? If you do not tell me why, I will kill you."

"I must hide because many people have made a conspiracy against me and I have many children to protect. I will not make war. I will give you seventeen bulls and five hundred bundles of *guinzé* to be pardoned."

"Granted," Kréan said. "From here to the shore of the sea, I command. I am the greatest of the chiefs, and if you disagree, I will kill you."

One day old Massawai did his sorcery in a lean-to. He wanted to fly like old Kréan. But old Kréan took the sorcery and said: "I will not kill you. I am God on earth and I do no harm. But I will take away your sorcery and you will never be able to do as I do until the end of the world."

And every night after that, old Massawai dreamed that Kréan was sleeping on the bed and Massawai under the bed. And old Kréan remained the greatest chief.

4

AN EXPLANATION OF DREAMS

If you dream of a serpent lying across the trail, it is very bad.

If you are dancing in the middle of a crowd, it is very good.

If you are talking to a black woman, it is good, above all if you must go on a trip.

If you are talking to a black man, it is very bad.

If you are talking to a white man, be careful. You must wash your gri-gri.

If you are talking to a white woman, it is very, very, very good.

If you see a white sheep with a black neck, if you see a bird-man and the gateway to the sacred wood, or if you see a gri-gri fly like an airplane with red fire, then you are sure to win. Because all that is the spirit of the gri-gri. That gives you strength.

If you dream that you have the medicine tunic and the trident in the midst of many people, then you will have many wives, many male children, and much happiness.

If you dream that when you blow into the Afwi's pot your voice is bad, the conspiracy is upon you. But if the voice is good, then the conspiracy is on your side.

If you are a witch-doctor and you dream that you are tattooing, then you will kill the evil sorcerer who is setting spells on you.

5

PRESS CLIPPING

from *La Guinée Française*, Conakry,
7 July 1953

The Court of Assizes of Guinea:

The 1953 session of the Court of Assizes of Guinea has come to a close with a particularly interesting affair that contrasts two societies very clearly. On the basis of our own moral principles, our code had to pass judgment on the traditions of old barbarian Africa.

We saw, during the course of this trial before a court grounded in European law, the surge of a very old world, of a law peculiar to the Toma, a law born of millennial custom, with which many witch-doctors of the forest are still impregnated. Eight defendants were present.

The eight prisoners denied any participation in any crime whatever, going so far as to assert that they did not know what a gri-gri was. . . . Unfortunately, autopsies have revealed the stripping away of certain pieces of flesh, always the same pieces, from the corpses. "The Toma chief Koiwogui," stated the prosecution, "had need of human flesh for a gri-gri that would give power, invisibility, and immunity to snake-bites."

Before the arrest of these merchants of the macabre, the district of Farakoro had become a region of Fear, where the natives left their villages only in armed groups. Since the arrests, it seems that calm has returned.

Here is the verdict:

"For murder, conspiracy to murder, and traffic in human flesh, the Toma chief Koiwogui, convicted ringleader, is sentenced to twelve years of hard labor and five subsequent years of exile; Koli Koiwogui, alias Agba Uri, and Wagbaoro Koiwogui, alias Tupu, the two killers, to eight years of hard labor and five subsequent years of exile; Soko Guilawogui and Gbou Koiwogui, six years of hard labor and five subsequent years of exile.

"Guards, take the prisoners."

6

THE SACRIFICE TO THE SERPENT

And then, when the great serpent comes to talk to me at night, in the morning I go to make the sacrifice:

One white rooster.

One sheep.

White kola nuts.

Ground white rice.

Sometimes there is the tom-tom, but no one sees the serpent.

Me, I see him: there is a place farther out that I know, where the serpent sleeps, but you cannot go there because the serpent does not want that and it is he who commands.

It is the same serpent that was with my grandfather that I know now.

APPENDIX

244

7

TO BE PROTECTED BY THE SERPENT

You go and hide in the bush.

If you see the serpent and his wife, you follow them.

When they couple, that takes a long time. You keep hidden. That can last several days. When it is finished, the serpent's wife cannot move. Then the serpent goes into the bush and collects leaves from trees he knows of.

You watch closely so as not to forget.

He comes back and puts the leaves on his wife. Then the serpent's wife begins to live again and they go off, both of them.

You come out of your hiding-place and you collect leaves from the same trees and you can make medicine with them. The serpent will help you and give you all his strength.

8

THE TRIAL OF POISON IMPOSED ON WITCH-DOCTORS DURING THE TATTOOING CEREMONIES

When the witch-doctor arrives for the tattooing with his gri-gri, they give him seven bundles of twenty *guinzés*.

They divide up the children to be tattooed.

All the gri-gris chant one by one. There are fifty or sixty of them.

A gift is given to the best.

The bulls are killed. A great bowl of red beans with meat in the middle, called *protowai*, is brought on. The greatest witch-doctor puts very strong poison in it, crocodile bile, and he says:

"Convoke all the devils. The best will eat from the great bowl where the poison is."

The Zogui spears a large piece of meat with his trident. He eats the crocodile bile. He doubles over six times. The seventh time it is all finished: he is through being sick. He says: "You can come and eat."

The others do not want to. "No. God gave it to you," they say. "We will not eat it."

The Zogui takes the rice and the gri-gri leaves.

"You can come and eat, all my children," he says. "You will not die."

His apprentices come and eat. They do not die.

The Zogui says to the others: "All those who came here with a gri-gri of their own must pay me a fine. Otherwise, because they did not want to eat from my bowl, I will cast a sickness spell on them."

The day of the tattooing, witch-doctors must not sleep on the ground.

9

WHY MEN MUST NOT TRUST WOMEN

A man and his wife, after walking a long time, came to the shore of the sea. They lived there happily.

One day a man who was a spirit arrived, covered with sores like a leper.

The woman did not want him to come into the hut, but the man himself cared for him and gave him food until he was cured.

Then he showed him the way back to the road and the two of them talked.

The woman followed them, hidden in the bush.

Before a great rock, the spirit stopped and said to the man:

"You will come back here alone. You will say the secret words and you will find little golden chairs and all wealth."

And then he disappeared. The woman went right back to the hut. That way the man did not know that she had followed him.

A boy came along, and while her husband was sleeping the woman told the boy everything and she wanted to take the treasure with her.

They went to the rock. They said the secret words, and they had all wealth, but the man came afterward and asked for the wealth in his turn.

And the spirit answered that he had already given everything.

And when the man went back to his hut, there was no one there any more.

That is why you should never trust women.

━━━ A NOTE ON THE TYPE

This book was set on the Linotype in Bodoni Book, *a printing-type so called after Giambattista Bodoni, a celebrated printer and type designer of Rome and Parma (1740–1813). Bodoni Book as produced by the Linotype company is not a copy of any one of Bodoni's fonts, but is a composite, modern version of the Bodoni manner. Bodoni's innovations in printing-type style were a greater degree of contrast in the "thick and thin" elements of the letters, and a sharper and more angular finish of details. The book was composed, printed, and bound by* KINGSPORT PRESS, INC., *Kingsport, Tennessee. Designed by* HARRY FORD.